RAILWAYS AROUN
HARROGATE

Volume Three

Martin Bairstow

D49 'Hunt' class No.62762 'The Fernie' pilots V2 No.60893 across Arthington Viaduct with the 9a.m. Liverpool-Newcastle on 4 August 1955. *(J. C. W. Halliday)*

Published by Martin Bairstow, 53 Kirklees Drive, Farsley, Leeds
Printed by Amadeus Press Ltd, Huddersfield, West Yorkshire

Introduction

First published in 1986, *Railways Around Harrogate* gave an outline history of the lines which once radiated from the town including the two routes which are still in operation. It was republished in 1989 with minor amendment by which time it has gained the suffix *Volume One*.

Volume Two appeared in 1988. It explored a number of themes in greater depth and was the first book in this series to introduce articles from guest contributors: 'By G5 to Otley' by Brian Sutcliffe, 'A Wharfedale Junction' by John G. Bradley and 'Wetherby in the 1940s' by Professor J. Allan Patmore. The book stretched the concept of 'Around Harrogate' by including a chapter on the Wensleydale Line from Northallerton to Garsdale.

Volume Three is an entirely new book which attempts to delve still further into the lines which have featured in the earlier two books. Again there are guest contributions. John Keavey tells us how he missed the last train from Pateley Bridge. Gerry Pierson recalls his days on the footplate at Starbeck Shed. Bill Smith tells us what he found on visits to Starbeck. He follows this up with a traffic report from the days when there was plenty of excursion business. Ted Barrington remembers his local station at Penda's Way whilst Richard Pulleyn offers pieces on the Thorp Arch Circular Railway and on the aftermath of the crash at Thirsk.

My own contribution includes Harrogate's place in the development of successive new types of railcar. I speculate on the exclusion of Harrogate from the present day 'Trans Pennine' network and question the wisdom of abandoning some of the rights of way. Wetherby may have had only 30 passengers in 1963 but could nobody foresee a time when things might have become very different. Apparently not, so we are left with several pages of pure nostalgia as Mike Mitchell and Peter Sunderland record on camera the Wetherby race traffic which used to instil life into this otherwise moribund backwater on a handful of days each year.

As always, I am grateful to everybody who has helped with the book. The articles and photographs are credited individually. The tickets were loaned by Geoffrey Lewthwaite. Most of the excursion leaflets are from the collection of David Beeken. John Holroyd helped with artwork and Glynis Boocok converted my scribble into a typed manuscript.

Farsley, Leeds
September 1998   Martin Bairstow

Contents

	page
The Last Train has gone	4
The Return of 'Mitchell/Illingworth'	8
Starbeck Shed 50D	12
Starbeck Locoman	14
A 1950s Traffic Miscellany	23
The 'Bradford Express'	29
Pioneer Railcars	32
Camping Coaches	40
Wayside Stations	42
Forgotten Junctions	46
Penda's Way	48
A Lost Commuter Route	51
Wetherby Race Traffic	57
The Thorp Arch Circular Railway	69
Emergency Diversionary Route	72
Trans Pennine to Harrogate?	77
Rights of Way	79

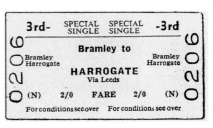

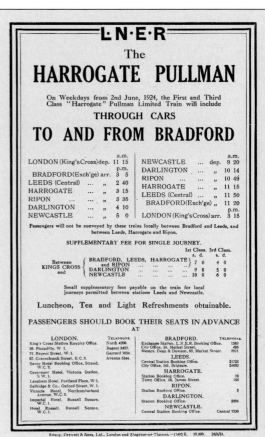

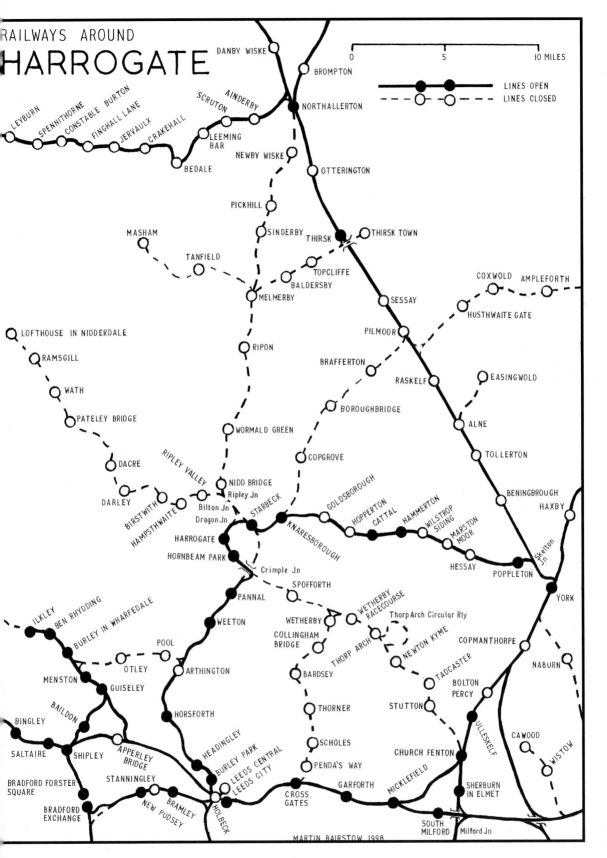

RAILWAYS AROUND
HARROGATE

MARTIN BAIRSTOW 1998

3

The last train has gone
By John Keavey

There was a whistle, a puff of smoke and the two coach train sped away from Pateley Bridge.
(David R. Smith Collection)

When the ominous Public Notices were finally posted, confirming that the Harrogate to Pateley Bridge branch was to be closed to passenger traffic, one problem remained. Some thought had to be given urgently of how best to arrange a first and a last ride on the line.

Harrogate was only a few miles away from my then home on Old Pool Bank – a mere thirty minutes run for a Cyclist like myself. So, on consulting "She who must be obeyed" and juggling the domestic arrangements for the advertised last day of service, it appeared that I could get myself to Harrogate in good time to catch the last train to Pateley Bridge – which if I recall correctly departed at 5.35pm (17.35 hours if you are a pedant!). I emphasise <u>to</u> because according to the Public Timetable the train never returned to base! A little application of applied logic suggested that it would in fact return – but as ECS, which means Empty Coaching Stock.

Next, with some urgency I wrote to British Railways' Holy of Holies at York enquiring if it would be possible to travel back on the ECS train if I paid of course the stipulated fare. BR North Eastern Region realised quickly that here was one way of slightly reducing the deficit being made on the line's operation and smartly replied 'yes'. Upon receipt of

the agreed special fare they would forward me a pass to travel back on the aforementioned train.

Came the appointed day and I rode gaily to Harrogate for my planned first and last train journey up Nidderdale. I locked the bike against a convenient cast iron pillar on the Station and went to the Booking Office for the ticket <u>to</u> Pateley Bridge (I already had my ticket <u>from</u> of course). Here, with the logic for which our Railways are famous, the Booking Clerk insisted on selling me a day return on the grounds that it was cheaper than the ordinary single ticket – and he wasn't there just to make more money for British Railways.

Grasping my ticket I then proceeded to the Barrier, when a Public Notice caught my eye informing me that for this day only a special train to Harrogate would return from Pateley Bridge and <u>Day Return Tickets</u> would be valid!!

I didn't say anything – I just thought it!

The last train was headed by a member of the ubiquitous G5 0-4-4T class of locomotive, which I was given to understand had trundled up and down Nidderdale now for several years – ever since it had ceased to travel to Ripon for the Masham Branch – an example by an earlier 'Beeching' in shutting LNER lines and stations.

4

We commenced our journey with the minimum of fuss, quietly slipping out of Harrogate and the clutches of the York line and making instead in the direction of Ripon, Thirsk, Northallerton and stations to Scotland. We built up a nice speed – thirty miles an hour at least, and clattered noisily over the points that permitted the "Old Road" to join us from Starbeck – the old Leeds Northern tracks. About four miles on our way we suddenly parted company with the line to the North and headed into the jaws of Nidderdale before slowing for a brief halt at Ripley Valley . . . which was a long walk from Ripley Village, which was why the suffix Valley was added.

Nidderdale is one of the lesser known Yorkshire Dales, but none the less a very attractive and scenic Dale, if a little hard to climb out of sometimes. There was now a string of attractive and near deserted wayside stations at which we had to call, and do virtually no business . . . places like Birstwith, Darley – Oh and Dacre which we learned was the Station for Brimham Rocks . . . we were not informed though that the Rocks were around a thousand feet above us!

Surprisingly little interest was shown by the local Populace, so perhaps British Railways had a point. A few peered suspiciously over the bridge parapets or leaned over fences, but in general our passage passed unnoticed.

Punctually at five past six we pulled into Pateley Bridge's single platform before a small knot of people who greeted us with an eye open for the Press photographer. One or two speeches were made, there was some shaking hands of the crew before the engine could be uncoupled to commence the familiar "running round" routine preparatory before returning for the last time to Harrogate. It was just about this time that I decided to take a picture – and retreated a short way up dale to the old level crossing which crossed the bottom of the High Street to join up with the erstwhile Nidd Valley Light Railway. I was just about to take the picture when there was a whistle, a puff of smoke, and the two coach train sped away from Pateley Bridge for the last time, carrying the valid day return passengers, of which there were several, but leaving stranded he

67253 had been the resident engine at Pateley Bridge for almost 33 years. Its longest absence had been in 1939 when it was sent away to be push-pull fitted.
(David R. Smith Collection)

Dacre, station for Brimham Rocks, in more prosperous North Eastern days.
(Peter E. Baughan Collection)

Speeches being made alongside the last train at Pateley Bridge. *(David Beeken Collection)*

67253 and the 'push and pull contraption' with which our contributor was 'evidently not acquainted'.
(J. W. Hague/David Beeken Collection)

who had purchased a special ticket to ride! I was mortified to say the least, but realized that I had only myself to blame – waiting for a push-pull loco to run round!

To add insult to injury I had an hour to wait for the West Yorkshire Bus back to Harrogate – my rail ticket was of course not valid on the bus, so I had to pay up again. At Harrogate an empty station indicated that the last train from Pateley Bridge had wasted no time in running for shelter at Starbeck or somewhere.

I expect you're thinking that I had a puncture next – well no, I had a pleasant ride back to Wharfedale, unsuccessfully racing a Leeds train between Rigton and Weeton, and all the while ruminating.

The plight of our contributor reached both the contemporary *Yorkshire Post* and the *Pateley Bridge & Nidderdale Herald*. From the latter we learn that his misfortune was compounded even further. The unnamed 'amateur photographer from Pool in Wharfedale being evidently not acquainted with the push and pull contraption' left his white mittens on the train. Happily he recovered them at Harrogate before cycling home.

47 years later we can reveal exclusively that the "amateur photographer" was none other than John Keavey, President of Embsay & Bolton Abbey Steam Railway.

The final journey at 5.35pm from Harrogate had carried over 100 passengers, including pressmen, enthusiasts, well wishers and officials such as Mr. A. Shea the shed master at Starbeck.

The driver was Mr Stanley Fletcher, age 49, a local councillor and magistrate, who had been at Pateley Bridge shed since 1926, first as a fireman and latterly as a driver. Addressing the crowd at Pateley Bridge, he declared that 'closing down the line will create great hardship for elderly people and for young mothers with prams who want to go shopping in Harrogate. This is a public service and ought to run as such. The solution might well have been to introduce inter availability of tickets between buses and trains and experiment with fares'. If this couldn't be done then he considered nationalisation a failure.

Other people thought that the answer lay in more trains and lower fares. A Mr E. H. Fawcett wrote to the Ripon & Pateley Rural District Council proposing a timetable of five return trips which would cater for 'workers, travellers, shoppers and pleasure seekers'.

The Clerk to Dacre Parish Council wondered whether there was any legislation which could be invoked compelling BR to provide the service. (Echoes of what happened a few years later on the Bluebell line). He wanted the Rural District Council to research the matter.

The leading campaigner against closure seems to have been Mr E. T. W. Addyman of Starbeck. He claimed that a steam train consumed £3 worth of coal getting from Harrogate to Pateley Bridge and back whereas a diesel railcar would be able to do it for 4s 7d. Mr Addyman was encouraged by a letter from the MP for Harrogate and by an invitation from the Central Transport Users' Consultative Committee to set out the requirements of Nidderdale residents. Even as the last train push-pulled away to the sound of seven exploding detonators, Mr Addyman shouted from his compartment 'don't give up hope'.

Even the Vicar of Pateley Bridge had something to say about the closure but we don't know what. He had written to the Prime Minister but was not prepared to reveal the contents of his letter unless and until Mr Attlee signified his consent to the correspondence being made public.

All honourable people, some maybe with ideas ahead of their time, but the tide would continue to flow against them for a long time to come.

Pateley Bridge engine shed which had been the home of No.67253 for most of the previous 33 years.
(Stephen Middleton Collection)

The Return of 'Mitchell/Illingworth'

'Illingworth' as Stephen Middleton hopes to have it looking. The name 'Mitchell' will appear on the other side as the present owner holds no views on what seems to have been a personality dispute in the Waterworks Department, back in 1930.

A brief outline history of the Nidd Valley Light Railway is given in *Volume One* with further photographs appearing in *Volume Two*.

From 1907 until 1929, Bradford Corporation operated a public railway for passengers and goods between Pateley Bridge and Lofthouse beyond which a contractors line continued another six miles to Angram Reservoir which was completed in 1915. The entire railway, public and private, was dismantled following completion of Scar House Reservoir, four miles beyond Lofthouse, in 1936.

'Mitchell/Illingworth' was a Hudswell Clarke 0-6-0 saddle tank built in 1916 for the Ministry of Munitions at whose Gretna factory it was numbered DES3.

After the War, it was bought by Bradford Corporation along with sister engine DES2 which was named 'Watson' after the recently deceased chief engineer of the Waterworks Department. DES3 was named 'Mitchell' after his successor. When Lewis Mitchell resigned in 1930, it was renamed 'Illingworth' after the Deputy Chairman of the Waterworks Committee. One can only assume that they had not parted on the best of terms.

Both 'Watson' and 'Mitchell/Illingworth' were vacuum fitted and could take their turn on passenger work including the through trains for workmen and families between Scar House and Pateley Bridge. They also performed on goods traffic both within the Scar House site and to and from Pateley Bridge.

In 1936, "Illingworth" returned to Hudswell Clarke in Leeds from where it was sold to McAlpines for use in building the Ebbw Vale steelworks where it carried the name 'Harold'. In 1940, it was sold to Mowlems who named it 'Swynnerton' whilst using it building the Royal Ordnance Factories at Swynnerton and Ruddington. In 1946 it was employed on the Workington Breakwater and later by Mowlems on Braehead power station near Renfrew.

By 1957 the loco was sold for scrap but it was never broken up. Eventually it was bought for preservation by Stephen Middleton of Harrogate. It is being restored for use on the Embsay & Bolton Abbey Steam Railway where it will carry the name 'Mitchell' on one side and 'Illingworth' on the other. It is hoped that it will work special trains with vintage six wheel coaches which Stephen Middleton is also restoring.

The Nidd Valley Light was the most remote railway in the Harrogate area and the first to close. Much of the course of the line can still be seen and the four stations survive as private houses.

'Watson' at Lofthouse Station about 1928. This engine subsequently worked on the construction of Ladybower Reservoir in Derbyshire. It ended up at Woolley Colliery near Barnsley, surviving until 1964.

(H. G. W. Household)

Ex-GWR steam railcar 'Hill' stands outside Pateley Bridge engine shed in 1928 alongside 'Blythe' which had been built new for the Nidd Valley in 1922.

(H. G. W. Household)

0-6-0T 'Milner' in Lofthouse Station. *(H.G.W. Household)*

'Milner' and 'Blythe' at the head of a goods train between Lofthouse and Scar House which also required two banking engines to keep it on the move. *(H. G. W. Household)*

Une semaine francaise à la gare d'Harrogate pendant les années cinquantes.

(Stephen Middleton Collection)

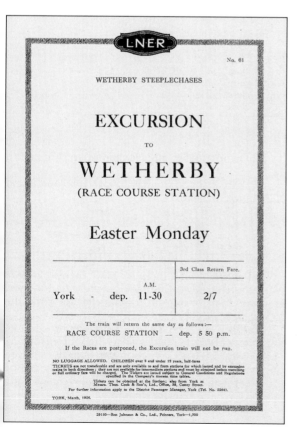

Starbeck Shed 50D
By F. W. Smith

Starbeck Shed on 12 September 1959 with J39 No.64861, two D49s, the leading one is 62759 'The Craven' and an ex-LMS 'Jinty' 0-6-0T.

(N. E. Stead)

Opened in 1857 and extended in 1864 and 1877, Starbeck was a two road straight shed open at both ends. A further extension was decided upon early in 1888 when accommodation was provided for two Midland Railway engines. There were further minor alterations around the turn of the century but otherwise the shed remained unaltered until closure apart from the new roof installed after the Second World War.

I visited Starbeck on Sunday 6 January 1946 and found the following engines on shed:

A6	4-6-2T	686/89/91/92/93/95
D20	4-4-0	708/25,1235/36/58,2014, 2105/07
G5	0-4-4T	468,580,1881
J39	0-6-0	1436/60/64/75/79/85/89.1532/34/60
J71	0-6-0T	299
J77	0-6-0T	166,954
N9	0-6-2T	1617/47

All the above were allocated to Starbeck. In addition there were three visiting engines: D20 No. 476 of Newport, K3 No. 1368 and V2 No. 4783 both of Gateshead. Sentinel railcar No. 2139 'Hark Forward' was derelict in a siding with the rails broken between the bogies.

The full Starbeck allocation at the end of the LNER period in December 1947 comprised 44 engines:

5	class	A6	4-6-2T
10	class	D20	4-4-0
6	class	D49	4-4-0
4	class	G5	0-4-4T
1	class	J24	0-6-0
12	class	J39	0-6-0
6	class	J77	0-6-0T

By October 1954, the allocation had dropped to 32.

I visited again on Sunday 3 April 1955 and found 33 engines on shed:

B16	4-6-0	61432/42/71
D49	4-4-0	62727/31/36/40/45/49/53/55/59/62/63/65/73/74
J39	0-6-0	64706,64818/45/47/55/57/59/66,64944
WD	2-8-0	90048/74/90,90461
J77	-6-0T	68392/93,68434

In February 1959 three ex LMS Stanier 2-6-4Ts were transferred to Starbeck but they had a short stay as they were all transferred to York the following May.

Starbeck Shed closed on 13 September 1959. 24 engines were transferred away including four ex LMS 'Jinty' 0-6-0Ts. The roof was quickly removed but the shed walls stood until partly demolished by the great gale of 1962. After that the remains were demolished and the site cleared.

A J25 on the original Leeds & Thirsk Railway, crossing over the East Coast Main Line on its way out of Thirsk Town, about 1950. *(Chris Wilson)*

An 'austerity' 2-8-0 with a northbound freight alongside the exchange siding for the narrow gauge Harrogate Gas Works Railway at Bilton Junction. The WD is setting back on to the Starbeck line in order to be overtaken by a passenger train. *(F. W. Smith)*

Class B16 No.61432 outside Starbeck Shed on 30 May 1959. *(M. Mitchell)*

Starbeck Locoman

By G. M. Pierson

Circumstances relating to 'who knew who and who would put a word in for you' dictated that I should commence my railway service as a cleaner at York rather than near my home at Starbeck.

Thus, on a bright midsummer morning, 21 June 1937, I reported to the shed for my first day as a cleaner and was soon engaged in burnishing a Class Z 'Atlantic' under the guidance of an 'old hand'. These 'old hand' cleaners were to be found at all LNER North Eastern Area sheds. Having joined the service in 1920-23 their promotion had been blocked by the Depression and in most cases they did not attain the status of fireman until 1940.

From 5 July the Summer working commenced and a good proportion of these seniors at York were syphoned off to Whitby and Scarborough to act as temporary, or 'red ink' firemen until the Winter. We juniors were split into two shifts, 8am and 1pm each alternate week and I initially fell on the 1pm turn. This was fortuitous as I was able to see the inaugural down and up Coronation streamliners.

Later that week I had my first firing turns, Thursday, Friday and Saturday on No.1 Up Goods pilot, tucked away in the ramifications of York Yard. If I remember correctly the locomotive was a Class J72, No. 2332. Other firing turns during that Summer were of a similar nature, interspersed with shed turns involving shunting locomotives and stabling engines, or 'wheeling them in', as it was referred to colloquially. I had about three turns on passenger or station pilots which suited me as one had ample opportunity to view the railway activity. I least enjoyed a couple of days spent on one of the warehouse pilots, where shunting was conducted between the confines of the wagon shops and the Engineer's Yard, out of sight to a great extent of the rest of the yards or main lines.

Running pilots, working between the various yards and to Dringhouses, were worked by Class A7 tank locomotives and J24/25 tender engines. I did not get any work on the former class but did on the latter type. I was working a turn of this nature when a driver first allowed me to take over the controls.

I had previously handled locomotives when on stabling duties. I would think that drivers thought they were safer on the ground directing operations than leaving it to us youngsters to direct them into a collision.

With the coming of Winter – except for a turn on the 'Loco Pilot' on Christmas Eve and a shed turn on New Year's Eve – firing was a non-starter.

In February 1938 I took up the offer of a mutual exchange of depots with a Starbeck cleaner, enabling me to live at home rather in lodgings.

It may be convenient here to look at some of the work performed at Starbeck, where the depot provided locomotives for the services around Harrogate and for some of the freight traffic handled in the marshalling sidings at Starbeck. The senior passenger link consisted of four turns covering:

1. Shed - Harrogate - West Hartlepool via Sinderby; West Hartlepool (Cliff House Sidings) - Thirsk - Starbeck (Freight) -Shed
2. Shed - Sidings - Starbeck(empty) - Harrogate - Leeds Central-Doncaster - Harrogate(1.40pm ex-Kings Cross) - Church Fenton and Wetherby; Harrogate - Starbeck Empty Stock (via Bilton Jct. to turn train) - Sidings - Shed;
3. Shed - Harrogate - York - Doncaster (The "Yorkshire Pullman"); Slow train Doncaster - Leeds Central - light engine to Leeds City then 5.22pm express - Harrogate - Starbeck(crew then worked forward to Knaresborough - Harrogate and to shed);
4. Shed - Harrogate - Leeds City (shunt as required), light engine to Leeds Central - Harrogate (The "Yorkshire Pullman") - Shunt train-Shed.

No. 1 would normally be a Class D21 or a B15. No. 2 was a D21. No.3 would be 2020, the rebuilt D20 allocated to Starbeck specifically for this train. No. 4 was usually a further D21. Spare D20s tended to cover for No. 4 and No. 3. D21s were not favoured for the Doncaster Pullman turn.

A second passenger link was the D20, consisting of seven double-manned turns covering a period of 14 weeks, during which each set of men would visit Hartlepool, Northallerton, Bradford, Selby and York.

One turn covering a 9am Ripon–Kings Cross train shunted at Copley Hill(GN) carriage sidings before returning home in charge of through coaches off the 10.10am ex-Kings Cross. The same locomotive was again at Leeds Central twice in the course of two trips covered by the late shift.

A sixteen week cycle covered by eight double-manned locomotives comprised the third or 'G5' link, in which activities embraced workings to Leeds, Bradford Forster Square, York, Pilmoor, Selby and Castleford.

Two Sentinel steam railcars, each worked by two shifts of men, were in service daily. The first confined its activities to plying between Harrogate and Knaresborough.

The second, which did not leave the shed until mid-morning, visited Leeds via Wetherby and then Ripon. At a later stage, it continued to Topcliffe to pick up workmen engaged on the construction of the RAF base. The second set of men on this turn worked to Wetherby and back then took up the Knaresborough service when the first car went on shed.

Two links catered for the freight operations. In the first of these, the drivers were immediately junior to those in the G5 link, whilst the firemen were senior to all the passenger firemen. The work covered by this link varied year by year as shown below:

	1937 Sign on	To
1	4.00am	Darlington
2	8.23pm	Stockton/Port Clarence
3	5.05am	Ripon pilot
4	9.55pm	Leeds (Armley Sidings)
5	11.11am	Ripon pilot
6	9.15pm	Leeds (Armley Sidings)

1939

2.23am	Newport
4.25am	Ripon pilot
8.10pm	Stockton/Port Clarence
6.25am	Darlington
10.00pm	Leeds (Armley Sidings)
8.45am	Darlington
11.11am	Ripon pilot

The Ripon pilot was normally a Sentinel loco (no. 92) so the firemen, who were not required, worked the early and late Harrogate pilot turns. Leeds (Armley) turns involved two return trips each (as did Armley–Starbeck turns worked by Leeds men).

The second goods link was the pick up or 'Old Man's' link:–

1937

Sign on	To
5.45am	Ripon/Thirsk
8.10am	Pateley Bridge
8.05am	Pilmoor
8.45am	Pool in Wharfedale
11.10am	Newby Wiske/Masham

1939

4.15am	Ripon–Starbeck–York–Starbeck
8.05am	Pilmoor
8.15am	Pateley Bridge
10.57am	Newby Wiske/Masham

The locomotive on the Pilmoor turn worked through to Newport, the men changing footplates en route for the return working.

Pilot turns in Starbeck Yards were normally covered by Class J77 tank locomotives working in the Down sidings (3 shifts), Up sidings (2 shifts) and in the North Yard/Warehouse. The fourth pilot in Harrogate Yard was a J25 tender engine with number 1743 allocated to this turn for most of the 1930s.

Not included above is a 9.35am Starbeck–Armley Goods, which was the outward leg of a Class D20 working. There was also a Mondays only 6.06am two trips to Armley turn covered by spare men and an afternoon cattle train running to Boroughbridge or to Knaresborough each alternate Monday. This latter working was again the province of spare men.

Reverting to my own experience at Starbeck, firing was initially confined to pilots and shed relief work. The latter was decidedly more onerous than at York, as it extended to cleaning smokeboxes, dropping fires and tipping coal hoisted on to the tenders by a steam crane which was of considerable age but remained in use until closure of the depot. Coupling up the coal tubs and releasing the catches, which held them central when they were being tipped, were operations fraught with hazard.

My first chance on the 'Main Line' came in June 1938, when I was billed to fire a return Harrogate–Liverpool excursion between Harrogate and Leeds. The locomotive provided was No. 824, a B15 4-6-0, with which Leeds men had brought the train earlier in the day. A large fire built up at Starbeck saw us to Harrogate with the empty stock and a couple or so charges en route took us to Leeds including the 1 in 94 ascent through Bramhope Tunnel. At Leeds we rapidly uncoupled and made our way to Neville Hill. We returned 'on the cushions' on the 9.47 from Leeds Central and

Sentinel car No.2268 'Emerald' crossing over at the north end of Ripon Station ready to work back to Harrogate.

(J. W. Hague/N. E. Stead Collection)

completed our shift on shed duties.

Another early trip was on No. 2101, Class D20, which involved working empty stock from Starbeck to Knaresborough and then to Leeds to shunt at Neville Hill. After coaling the engine we proceeded to Leeds City to work the 1.48pm express to Harrogate, where we were relieved by the second set who would work to West Hartlepool and back. This was my first experience of the heavy grind of five miles from Holbeck almost to Bramhope Tunnel and gave me an inkling of what was involved in the day to day work of the passenger link men.

A first taste of the Pateley Bridge pick-up found me on J21 No. 973. This was a far better engine than her sister, 1811, on which I had my first trip to Bradford taking an empty train which we returned as a Bradford–York race special. We were relieved at Starbeck to undertake the inevitable shed duties. Oddly enough on the corresponding 'Ebor' day in 1939, I was again on a race special with a J39 from Gorton Shed this time light engine to Ilkley, where we took over a special from Barrow-in-Furness to York from a Midland 4F, running non-stop to the former Holgate Race Course platform. Our engine was deposited at York shed and we returned home as passengers to the usual shed duties.

Again on 973 was a trip via Wetherby to Leeds and back the same way on a turn that ran in lieu of a Saturdays excepted Sentinel Car working. Having disposed of 973 we were despatched to Harrogate to relieve the men on a Saltburn–Leeds train which arrived in the charge of a D17 4-4-0. This trip to Leeds was my only outing on that class, of which three were still active as cover for D20s at the LNER outstation at Manningham Midland depot. The latter closed in October 1938 and the D17s were then taken away for scrapping.

Another memory of 1938 is working a 7.25pm Leeds special (two trips to Armley) with No. 1743. This was the J25 normally confined to Harrogate pilot duty but she performed quite well. Q6 or A7 tank engines were the norm for Armley turns. The latter had played a very prominent part on this work until the late 1930s. Towards the close of 1938 the Leeds and Starbeck contingents of A7s were transferred to Teesside, where it was intended they should cover trip working between West Hartlepool and Newport yards, I think this was to facilitate a reduction in marshalling at the Hartlepool end.

Highlights in 1939 included working a G5 to York on an ordinary service then, after a long wait, picking up a return Sunday School Special to work up the main line to Pilmoor, and thence to Boroughbridge and empty stock home. Dashing up the Main Line with express headlights on a small engine savoured of the early days when old Class 901 and Tennant Class 2-4-0 engines held sway.

There was a vast volume of excursion work on both Saturdays and Sundays before the 1939 War, including the popular evening excursions. Starbeck engines and men took a share in this work, often relieving Newcastle men at Harrogate to work forward to Leeds and back. On Summer Saturday men were loaned to Leeds to cover workings Newcastle or Saltburn almost on a regular basis.

My swansong as a Fireman in the first week of the War, before the Emergency Time-table came into force, was a day on the Ripon–Leeds Copley Hill shunt D20 turn.

On the final Saturday of the normal timetable worked the late Ripon pilot on our friend 973. This was standing in for the Sentinel which, incidentally never reappeared, as the wartime traffic at Ripon was rather too heavy for a Sentinel shunter.

The war brought about enormous change everywhere, some of which had lasting effect on the working at Starbeck. The running of specials to Heaton on Tyneside, when our men change footplates en route, soon brought K3 2-6-0s a regular visitors. The class had not been unknown at Starbeck by any means but tended to be uncommon on shed. This was not the whole picture, however and within a few weeks we were playing host to V2 regularly and the occasional A3.

Resumption of near normal local services on December 1939 saw me firing a D20 on Bradford–Northallerton turn, and from that time on except for Boxing Day – I was firing continuously until actually appointed a Fireman in June 1940.

At that time two flows of freight traffic sustained the marshalling facilities at Starbeck, namely through traffic exchanged between Leeds or beyond and the North and local traffic channelled via either Leeds or York. Centre of operations was at Armley Sidings, where a large volume of the traffic passing through Starbeck was exchanged with the West Riding/Bradford area of the GN section or with the LNWR line of the LMS Railway. Limited accommodation at Armley precluded any intensive sorting of traffic, hence the facilities developed at Starbeck, where a commodious Down Yard assembled trains for the North. To the South of the engine shed were the Up sidings where Leeds bound traffic was sorted.

Beyond the junction with the York line and the passenger station was the North Yard. At this latter site there was an extensive warehouse where a huge volume of tranship activity took place. The yard also served as a local goods and coal depot and for the marshalling of outward-bound pick-up trains. An early wartime measure was an input of warehouse traffic off the GC line, which was diverted into Starbeck to relieve pressure on York. Two Class A freight tank locos were sent to the depot to cover the working of this traffic from Milford Junction via Church Fenton and Harrogate. It is thought that two return trips to Milford per shift was the intended working to bring in this traffic but such an arrangement did not always materialise.

Freight trains passing through Harrogate Station had been almost a novelty before 1940. In 1939 these were confined to a Starbeck–Gascoigne Wood coal empties train at about 9.30 each morning. This was invariably worked by a Selby Class Q7 loco which arrived in the area heading the 5.00am loaded mineral from Gascoigne Wood via York. A loco off a mid-morning York–Starbeck–Harrogate freight took a Starbeck–Neville Hill load through the town around 1.00pm, the loco in this case varying from a J26 to a B15/B16.

There was in addition a Q6 hauled Neville Hill freight and a corresponding return working during mid-afternoon. This was followed by a Selby J25/J26 loco in charge of a pick-up off the Church Fenton branch which retraced its route shortly afterwards, frequently calling at Harrogate Station to detach gas tanks or miscellaneous vehicles.

By the onset of the 1950s the scene was completely changed. There was a frequent flow of freight trains through Harrogate, day and night, usually double headed between Bilton and Wetherby or Neville Hill, according to their destination. The direct Leeds–Starbeck line had ceased to function as a freight link with the North, use being confined to the passage of a daily pick-up worked by Neville Hill depot and tanker traffic between Haverton Hill and Heysham which took the North to West curve at Arthington.

The section of line between Pannal Junction and Starbeck was closed in May 1951 and subsequently lifted. This residual traffic then ran via Harrogate. At Starbeck activity was reduced to the sorting of local traffic and crippled wagons, the latter brought into the area for grading which was carried out in the Up Sidings.

These changes had originated in wartime developments. Initially, in February 1940, traffic between the North and the GC Section in block loads for Mottram, Annesley, or Banbury, was diverted from the main line to run via Ripon, Harrogate and the Church Fenton branch to Milford Junction where it was staged for forward working until there was a balancing flow of northbound traffic. Milford represented a suitable turn round point for GC

workings and had indeed in pre-Groupings days represented the northern limit of GC running powers in respect of freight traffic. Due to the heavy gradients both North and South of Harrogate double-heading was necessary in both directions between Bilton Junction and Wetherby. There were also two or three Normanton trains diverted over the same route, often conveying iron ore empties south and loaded ore on the return. At the outset conductor drivers and guards were provided to and from Bilton, but from June 1940, re-manning became the established method of working. Certain northbound workings from Starbeck Yard involved a change of footplates en route, possibly at Wiske Moor, for example, where Starbeck men would take over a southbound train for Milford, from whence they would return home with a load for Starbeck.

An early personal experience of such a working involved a J39 outward and change over to a C7 Atlantic to work to Milford. A few months after the Milford and Normanton workings were established LNWR traffic was diverted to Neville Hill in place of Armley, enabling this to be worked direct to the North via Wetherby and Harrogate. The provision of assisting engines was involved, with Starbeck and Neville Hill sharing the work.

A further development around this time was coal traffic between the North East and Lancashire via Starbeck. This arrived in one load which was split into two trains for forward working to Neville Hill via Arthington and across Leeds. Northbound empties travelled out of Leeds via the Wetherby route. At a subsequent stage these trains were re-routed to Colne via Arthington and Ilkley and worked there as double-headed single loads. Starbeck men had already added Skipton to their sphere of operation some time previously, when coke from the Durham area for Barrow had begun to be routed via Starbeck and the Wharfedale line. Throughout the War period and beyond, a considerable petrol tank traffic

Disused since 1951, Crimple Low Viaduct on the original Leeds & Thirsk Railway between Pannal and Starbeck, can be approached by footpath and is just visible from trains crossing the larger Crimple Viaduct. *(F. W. Smith)*

was dealt with for an extensive Air Ministry depot opened in 1939 between Dragon Junction and Starbeck North. This often absorbed two full train loads in little over 24 hours.

Measures to cater for all the additional traffic included a down loop at Melmerby, conversion of the up long siding at Ripon into a loop, and provision of a new signal box and up loop at Monkton Moor between Ripon and Wormald Green Stations. Similar up and down loops were constructed at Bilton, together with a facing connection off the down line into the gas company's sidings, where banking engines were usually berthed between duties. A banker spur was also constructed on the up Starbeck line at Bilton, but its utilisation was a figment of the planners' imagination.

Recollections of personal involvement in this wartime scene would fill a book. Early experiences in 1940 included a first trip up the Masham branch on a Selby Q7, which on that particular day had failed at Starbeck on the Gascoigne Wood coal train job. A few weeks later I was on the branch again on a somewhat down-at-heel D20, afflicted with a non-stop Westinghouse brake pump which caused the driver to remark that his head was buzzing. He was not alone.

We had a similar foreign D20 on the Otterington pick-up, a turn involving a change of footplates en route with Newport men. They were not at all chuffed when they met us with their J24, especially as our morning departure time had become somewhat advanced and they had come a lot further than Otterington. Delayed departures were not uncommon at that time due to non-availability of motive power.

Amid a fair share of shed relief and pilot work there was much opportunity to try my hand on a variety of passenger turns on the various G5, D20 and D21 class locomotives, the last displaying a fair appetite for coal without comparable results. The hardest turn with G5 engines involved working the 09.40 Stockton on Tees train between Leeds and Harrogate hauling a set of five Gresley bogies non-stop after calling at Holbeck.

The only time I worked this turn, No. 580 was pressed hard on the climb to Horsforth but it responded well to 'little and often' firing, and we topped the bank with a reasonable water level to coast through Bramhope Tunnel and have a good head of steam available when power was applied again for the final dash to Harrogate. Being a Saturday, the shift was rounded off with a return trip to Pilmoor on the lunchtime Saturdays only service. Within a few months this turn had been transferred into the D20 link.

June 1940, saw my appointment as a regular fireman and I was placed in the Push-Pull link which embraced two turns. Both involved working to Pilmoor and back, then to Bradford and back, followed, on the late shift, by three return trips to Knaresborough. Our regular engine, the only available Push-Pull fitted loco, was 387, noteworthy for her extended tanks, a feature giving rise to a frequent tendency to run hot – hence the occasional use of ordinary G5 0-4-4Ts.

After some three months I was promoted to the G5 link on 408, where I only stayed a very short while before a further move, into the D20 link.

Initiation in this link was on a rather heavy turn. After working the 06.30 via Arthington to Leeds City, where our load was made up to 10 bogies, we plodded all stations to Selby via Wetherby and Church Fenton. The additional stock attached at Leeds was required for the conveyance of an army of workmen engaged in the construction of the extensive ordnance complex at Thorp Arch. Turn-round time at Selby was minimal, and it later became the practice to change footplates with Bridlington men for the return working which followed the same path. Midweek on this turn, the final leg of the programme was the 12.57 slow from Leeds, but on Saturdays it was the 12.20 express followed by a Saturdays only trip to Pateley Bridge and back to round off the shift and ensure that the fire was well and truly solid with clinker! Our regular locomotive was 2014, not the best of steamers. At various times we had other locomotives due to repairs or traffic requirements.

One turn comprised two trips to Leeds culminating with the working of the 1.48pm Leeds to Stockton on Tees, which ran express to Thirsk, then all stations. This train merited something larger than a D20 and other types were provided. The late shift men took over at Harrogate and worked through to West Hartlepool and back. In a typical week on the late turn we had No. 111 – a G.N. Section K3, a V2, C7 Atlantic, D21 and a further Atlantic finishing the week on 4006, one of the original K3s still having a G.N. style cab.

Once, on a York turn we had to relinquish a D21 due to a minor defect. We were given a G.C. D9 Class 4-4-0 to work back to Harrogate and then to Leeds and back. The arrival of this D9 invoked great interest among the spotters at Harrogate.

Such was life in the D20 link, but early in December 1941, further promotion took me into the banker and pick-up link, manned by the most senior drivers, and embracing some 14 turns all round the clock. Five A8 4-6-2T locomotives were allocated for banking duties, namely 1326, 2145, 1502, 1527 and 1531. Of these, from a fireman's viewpoint, 1326 and 2145 were non-starters and 1527 indifferent. Only the other two were reliable steamers. Popular locomotives were two A7s (later four of this class), whilst B15s, J21s and even N8 0-6-2T 348 were utilised at various times. The gradient from Bilton to Harrogate was 1 in 66, followed by a sharp dip south of Harrogate and then some five miles of down gradient, terminating in another dip before Wetherby West Junction.

The two dips in the profile of the route were the cause of quite a number of breakaways and necessitated careful handling of any loose coupled trains. The Ripon-Harrogate-Church Fenton line was

39 No.64942 approaching Harrogate Station from the north with a mixed freight in the early 1950s.
(J. W. Hague/David Beeken Collection)

6-2 No.2404 'City of Ripon' leaving Ripon northbound about 1936 *(J. W. Hague/N. E. Stead Collection)*

a favoured route for troop trains in both directions. Whilst Up trains could rush the bank into Harrogate, Down trains were assisted from Wetherby to Harrogate. Although not equipped with train brakes, there was no hesitation in the use of A7 locomotives for such work if they happened to be the available banker. When heading a V2 hauled troop train, their small wheels would be going at a fair rate of revolutions in the Wetherby–Spofforth dip.

On the pick-up workings in the link, a wide variety of locomotives were employed. Amongst various strangers, I fired one of the two original B1(later B18) ex-GC 4-6-0s on the Masham branch and an ex-GC B7 on the Pilmoor pick-up. In one week on the Pateley turn, power varied from a C7 Atlantic to a G5 on the Saturday.

During this period Tanfield and Masham stations became railheads for a huge volume of ammunition which was stored along the lanes in the locality. This traffic necessitated two trains daily on the Masham branch, usually worked by J39/Q6 locos with Class 04 and other types appearing at various times.

The contour of the branch followed an undulating course not very conducive to easy working of the heavy and lengthy trains which the traffic called for. The existence of three level crossings between Melmerby Junction and Tanfield, to be approached at 10mph after sounding the engine whistle was a further hindrance.

Given a somewhat over eager approach by elderly drivers, conditioned by many years on passenger work, it is not surprising that no set of gates came through the War without serious injury. On the afternoon turn the guard was required to pick up water supplies at Melmerby for distribution to each of the gatehouses located at these crossings. One afternoon we were on the steep ascent to Tanfield, passing over the preceding crossing with a jag of empty box vans. My driver kept enquiring if

we had cleared the gates and was the guar stopping us. When the latter did eventually sign us to stop, the regulator was shut and the stear brake applied in what can only be described as on simultaneous movement as a result of which th rebound of our load took away the gates which ha been replaced over the line with an unfortunat degree of promptitude.

In 1943 a considerable reshuffle of motive pow took place in the North Eastern Area and some of th variety of locomotives in use at various depo diminished. Freight locomotives became categorise as Main Line or Local, the former continuin somewhat as 'Common Users' and the latter confine to out and home or purely local workings. A larg number of N E 'Atlantics' which had been familiar o freight workings were banished to the Hull Distric ceasing to appear on the Milford circuit.

The large allocation of J39s and the older Q5 0-8 0s, long familiar on workings to and from Teessid were replaced by additional Q6 locomotives with th Leeds allocation of that class also vastly increase Starbeck gained five J21s, three B15 and three N locomotives. At the same time Austerities and US 2-8-0 locomotives appeared on the scene and he sway on through workings for some months unt 'called up' in time for D Day. On home groun within a short time, an influx of J39s supplanted th J21s at Starbeck and from then on monopolise local work right into the 1950s.

Around 1944 the 'Old Man's Link' was split u and I fell into a small link comprising two Masham two Pilmoor, a Pateley Bridge and a Leeds turn, tw sets of men each sharing a J39, on an 'owner-drive basis with 1460 as our engine.

Summer 1945 saw promotion into the 'Bilton' lin working to Darlington, Milford and Teesside. Th was the time when the War Department and US. locomotives had vanished abroad and Q

The demolition gang hav done a more effective job o the gates at Tanfield than wa ever achieved by firema Pierson or his driver. Th rotating board signal show that the crossing is closed t rail traffic.

(F. W. Smith Collectio

locomotives were in evidence, but Darlington turns in particular afforded the opportunity to sample a wider variety of types including V2s. Banker engines had by then changed. All but one of the ten Class A6 'Whitby Tanks' had supplanted the A8 and A7s in March 1945. They remained at Starbeck, although in reduced numbers, until the early 1950s when J39s took over.

For the Autumn I fell back into the J39 link on 1460 again, by which time an afternoon Ilkley trip had replaced the pm Pilmoor turn. A big RAF ammunition dump on the branch had justified the two turns previously in operation.

A return to the more senior link in January 1946 coincided with the 'demob' of Austerity locomotives. A large number became based at Newport and Neville Hill depots. Our range of activity embraced Darlington, Stockton-on-Tees, Newport, Normanton, Milford, Leeds and Colne. In addition, towards the end of 1946, Doncaster was added to the sphere of our duties by the diversion of three Low Fell–Whitemoor trains via Harrogate, Church Fenton and Knottingley with a varying selection of locomotives.

Starbeck men working these trains were billed to change footplates with Doncaster men en route at Church Fenton but this arrangement rarely materialised. In my experience, on the next occasion we did have to change over, the engine we took was – guess what – streamlined A4 No. 1 'Sir Ronald Matthews' newly off plant and resplendent in a first post-War repaint in LNER blue livery. A little earlier a friend of mine had A2 'Mons Meg' off works in the same way.

Another class of locomotive frequently encountered in the link at this period was the LNER-operated Stanier 8F with which we became quite familiar. A curiosity of the War years is that I know of only one instance of an LMS locomotive being seen at Starbeck when a 4F passed through with a troop train for Thirsk.

After four years in this interesting link, eyesight failure took me off footplate duties, much to my regret. Thereafter I viewed activity through an office window.

In a transitional period, 1948-50, D49 'Hunt' Class locomotives had taken over most of the passenger work at Starbeck, this being on a much reduced scale than in 1939. These were mainly from Leeds, where they had been displaced by B1s. Their range of activities in the hands of Starbeck men came to include Hull and Leeds–Bradford Forster Square by the Midland route.

Other turns embraced the York-Leeds line. There was the 'Yorkshire Pullman' to work to and from Leeds Central. Otherwise; except for a morning Leeds–Middlesbrough service, they were confined to the Northallerton–Leeds line and one double-shifted turn to Bradford via Otley.

'Austerity' 2-8-0 No.90503 crossing Ripon Viaduct with the Heysham to Tees Yard ammonia tank train.
(J. W. Hague/N. E. Stead Collection)

Class G5 engines disappeared from the scene with the closure of the Pilmoor line to passenger traffic in 1950 and the Pateley branch likewise the following year.

On the freight side, J39s, prevailed, supplemented by three Austerity 2-8-0s which catered for the tanker traffic that had arisen between Haverton Hill and Heysham via Skipton. A further Austerity turn was a night goods to Gascoigne Wood via York, returning with loaded coal via Wetherby. A lunch-time turn covered mineral empties to Gascoigne Wood via Harrogate. There were still a number of Bilton turns to Gascoigne Wood rather than to Milford, and the staff continued to participate in northbound traffic to some degree. This pattern of freight working persisted until closure of the depot in 1959.

Excursion working, though never of the magnitude of pre-War days, had resumed with Starbeck men frequently working to the Yorkshire Coast with trains which they worked as empty stock to and from Bradford Forster Square. A regular Summer Saturday holiday train from Teesside to Blackpool commenced in June 1946, Starbeck men taking over at Harrogate and working to Colne, where LM power took over.

The engine was turned at Colne to await a return train which they worked to Harrogate and a further set of Starbeck men took over to work northwards.

Originally a B16 or K3 working, this train was usual in the hands of a B1 during the 1950s. Eventual our men were working through to Blackpool ov this route with excursions during Illumination tim with, of course, LM Region conductors beyon Colne. B16 No. 1442, later 1478, was allocated Starbeck and shared the work of the WD engines.

The Masham branch came to be covered by th Ripon pilot engine, which made a trip up the branc each afternoon, Saturdays excepted. Initially an A had taken over the work at Ripon, but later on J3 prevailed.

When the second wave of dmus entered traffic 1956, Starbeck men took a share of the work. Stea passenger work declined rapidly leaving only th Pullman and Kings Cross through services to b catered for. In the final year of the depot, three LM 2-6-4Ts came on the scene to cater for this residu work. 'Hunts' continuing to share the work wer frequently to be found as banking engines at Bilto

With closure in September 1959, remainin steam working on branches was allocated to Nevi Hill and York. Through traffic via Bilton an Wetherby was diverted via the Main Line and Yor Shunting at Harrogate, Ripon and – for a sho period – at Starbeck was undertaken by diese based at Harrogate Station. Thus the curta descended on a once busy area of operation.

J39 No.64818 emerging from Wormald Green Tunnel with a Saturday pick-up goods from Ripon to Starbeck on 20 February 1954.
(J. W. Hague)

A 1950s Traffic Miscellany
By F. W. Smith

Ex-GWR railcar No.20 shunting its low loader wagon at the south end of Harrogate Station during trials on 24 August 1952.
(H. Whitby/S. Askew Collection)

Great Western diesel railcar No. 20 was used for trials between Leeds and Harrogate on 24 August 1952. The car ran in high gear for the first two trips. The booked times for the 18 miles were 27 minutes down with three speed restrictions, and 24 1/2 minutes up with two restrictions. The third run was made hauling a four wheel van on the same schedules. The fourth trip had a long low wagon in tow increasing the weight by ten tons. The down run on this occasion was made in 30 minutes (schedule 31 1/2) with the car in low gear throughout. The return journey was booked for 26 1/2 minutes back to Leeds. The driver for the day was from Reading. Neville Hill shed supplied a conductor.

The same car commenced trials from Boston shed in Lincolnshire for four days beginning 30 September 1952. No. 20 survives on the Kent & East Sussex Railway where a virtual total rebuild is nearing completion.

It was customary on bank holidays to augment services to popular destinations like Harrogate and Knaresborough. On 3 August 1954 (Bank Holiday Tuesday) N1 0-6-2T No. 69445 worked from Leeds Central to Harrogate relieving one of the diesel trains.

Easter Monday 11 April 1955 was fine and sunny. The planned diesel service between Bradford Exchange and Knaresborough was abandoned and all the diesel sets were used to provide an enhanced frequency between Leeds and Knaresborough. Even this was insufficient and some additional steam trains had to be run. Three reliefs, each consisting of 11 coaches, were worked by J39 No. 64855, B16 No. 61433 and a D49. Of greater interest, however, were a five coach special hauled by N1 No. 69484 of Ardsley shed and a four coach working behind J6 0-6-0 No. 64276, possibly the first visit of a J6 to Harrogate.

Traffic was again too much for the diesel sets over Whitsun 1956. On Whit Monday over 10,000 people used the service between Bradford, Leeds, Harrogate and Knaresborough. Two dmu sets were brought from Tyneside to reinforce the West Riding fleet of eight two car formations. A half hourly service of four car trains was run between Bradford and Knaresborough but this was insufficient to cope. Scheduled reliefs were worked by N1 tanks and 0-6-0s Nos 64173 and 64286. 64173 and N1 No. 69467 worked one nine coach train tender to bunker. Yet more capacity was improvised with extra workings hauled by a J39 and D49 No. 62773 'The South Durham' which ran via Wetherby.

In those days there was plenty of spare capacity available for working special traffic. On Saturday 26

'Hunt' class No.62755 'The Bilsdale' and J39 No.64922 with empty stock at Ripon about 1955.

(J. W. Hague/N. E. Stead Collection)

J39 No.64944, of Starbeck Shed, prepares to leave Harrogate with at least ten coaches for Leeds.

(J. W. Hague)

March 1955, 52 excursions were run for the FA Cup semi finals to Birmingham (Sunderland v Manchester City) and Sheffield (York City v Newcastle United). A total of 587 coaches were required. 11 of the trains from Sunderland and Newcastle ran via Ripon and Leeds, the rest via York and Rotherham. They were worked exclusively by class V2 2-6-2s – no less than 31 of them.

A week later three 'black fives' Nos. 45101, 45201 and 45218 appeared at Headingley with excursions from Castleford for the Rugby League Cup semi final. They worked their empty stock on to Starbeck but 45218 had to be assisted out of Headingley by a B16.

Compound 4-4-0 No. 41061 found itself shunting at Ripon all morning on 1 February 1955. It had been called out to assist B1 No. 61061 which had failed at Melmerby with a morning train to Leeds but it was not required. The Ripon yard pilot, J39 No. 64859 took the train on instead.

The 8.55am Newcastle to Liverpool often required the help of a pilot engine between Ripon and Leeds. Usually the assistant was a Starbeck D49 but on 19 March 1955 D20 No. 62384 was coupled onto A2 No. 60517 'Ocean Swell'. The D20 was a Selby engine which had worked the early morning train for workmen from Doncaster to the Thorp Arch complex.

On 20 December 1955 an exceptionally heavy snow storm caused chaos in the Harrogate, York and Leeds districts. The position was most severe at York owing to the keen detection on the electric signalling installation there. Main line passenger trains were diverted between Northallerton and Doncaster via Melmerby, Harrogate, Church Fenton, Burton Salmon and Knottingley to Shaftholme Junction. WD 2-8-0 No. 90076 was sent out to assist southbound sleeping car trains if required. Goods traffic was virtually at a standstill, the backlog not being cleared until 27 December when four Newport to Neville Hill specials were run.

After the end of the Second World War, weekend and bank holiday excursions from Bradford Forster Square to the North East recommenced via Otley and Harrogate. On Easter Sunday, 1 April 1956, 'Crab' 2-6-0 No. 42770 hauled an excursion from Bradford to Newcastle. It was worked by Manningham men with a Starbeck conductor from Harrogate. The following Saltburn excursion consisting of five coaches was hauled by Ivatt 2-6-0 No. 43044 as far as Harrogate where it was joined on to the Leeds-Saltburn train. The same day 'Black Five' 4-6-0 No. 44733 worked a Blackpool to York excursion via Ilkley and Harrogate. It was assisted by Ivatt 2-6-2T No. 41326 from Skipton as far as Otley.

On 10 May 1956, A2 4-6-2 No. 60524 'Herringbone' on the southbound 'Queen of Scots Pullman' failed at Ripon with leaking tubes. It was replaced by J39 No. 64942, commandeered off the Masham branch goods. This loco was not thought to be man enough for the job so it waited for sister engine No. 64821 to arrive light engine. The Pullman then departed double headed after a stand of about one hour.

Engines working inbound excursions from the London Midland Region occasionally failed at

A1 No.60154 'Bon Accord' passing Arthington with the Sunday 5p.m. Manchester Exchange to Newcastle on 2 June 1957. *(B. K. B. Green)*

Two J39s, 64821 and 64942 pause at Ripon with the southbound 'Queen of Scots Pullman' on 10 May 1956. *(J. W. Hague/N. E. Stead Collection)*

J39 No.64861 pilots B1 No.61016 'Inyala' on the 8.55a.m. Newcastle to Liverpool as they pass Dragon Junction and attack the final 1 in 66 into Harrogate on 21 December 1957. *(M. Mitchell)*

A3 No.60036 'Colombo' coming off Arthington Viaduct with a northbound express in 1955. *(J. C. W. Halliday)*

'Black Five' No.44824 ascending the spur from Gelderd Junction towards Leeds Central with the 12.50 Harrogate to King's Cross on 18 February 1967. The train would be diesel hauled from Leeds.

(D. J. Mitchell)

Harrogate. Starbeck shed usually provided a replacement or assisting engine as far as Skipton for the return journey, most Starbeck men knowing the road that far. On 24 May 1956 'Jubilee' class No. 45640 'Frobisher' arrived with a special from Carlisle. Both injectors were faulty and could not be repaired in time for the return trip so B16 No. 61432 was provided to assist it back to Skipton where a replacement engine took over. Only two days later, a Carlisle engine No. 44676 worked an Ayr to Harrogate excursion via Ilkley. On arrival it was a complete failure with melted metal on one of the right hand tender wheel bearings. J39 No. 64791 was given to the Manningham men for the return journey as far as Skipton.

There were many occasions when main line traffic was diverted from Northallerton to York via Ripon, Bilton Junction and Starbeck. This happened on 9 and 16 September 1956 due to track work between Pilmoor and Raskelf. 16 expresses were diverted on the first date and seven of these were given assistance by Starbeck D49 engines such as 62736 'The Bramham Moor' piloting A4 No. 60011 'Empire of India'. On 16 September some B16s were used with 61436 piloting A3 No. 60075 'St. Frusquin' and 61478 with A3 No. 60064 'Tagalie'.

Harrogate had a very unusual visitor on 15 May 1957 when the 1950 built North British diesel electric No. 10800 hauled a six coach special from Harrogate to Lincoln and back via Church Fenton and Shaftholme Junction in connection with the Ruston centenary conference. The loco returned light to Derby the next morning.

What was believed to be the first to the area by a 'Clan' class locomotive took place on Sunday 30 June 1957 when 4-6-2 No. 72003 'Clan Fraser' worked an excursion from Blackpool to York and back via Colne, Skipton, Ilkley, Otley and Harrogate.

30 June 1957 was also the last day for the two Sunday trains which had run between Leeds City and Skipton via Otley and Ilkley. 'Black Five' No.

45489 worked the final turn at 6.57pm from Skipton. It slipped to a stand as it tried to pull away from Arthington and had to be banked up the 1 in 94 through Bramhope Tunnel by D49 No. 62758 'The Cattistock' which was detatched from the 8.15pm Harrogate to Leeds. 62758 returned to its own train which it got underway 45 minutes late. There was serious delay to other trains as well.

The following week saw the introduction of an hourly Sundays only diesel service through from Castleford to Ilkley via Leeds Central and Otley with three workings extended to Bolton Abbey.

The Royal Train visited Harrogate on 10 July 1957 in connection with the Great Yorkshire Show. It was worked from Leeds to Harrogate and then on to York by B1 4-6-0s 61176 and 61224.

In June 1958, five standard 2-6-4 tanks were transferred to Neville Hill to replace withdrawn D49s. They were soon to be found working from Leeds to Harrogate, Ripon and Northallerton, the first tank engines to be used in regular traffic north of Harrogate for many years.

A very unusual engine on a passenger turn was class 9F 2-10-0 No. 92169 which worked the 9.38 South Shields to Manchester and back via Ripon, Harrogate and Leeds on Saturday 13 September 1958.

During October 1958, new Metrovic Co-Bo diesels made trial runs from Stockton to Leeds, out via Wetherby returning via Arthington. On 7 October the loco was D5703 with 13 coaches. The run on 13 November came to grief when D5705 failed at Wormald Green with a blocked fuel injection pump and had to be rescued by the Ripon pilot engine, J39 No. 64847.

From 2 February 1959, the night shift was cut out at signal boxes on the direct route between Leeds and Harrogate, a move which had been threatened for sometime. As a result, two early morning and one late evening trains were diverted via Wetherby without stopping at any intermediate stations.

Metrovic Co-Bo No.D5705 approaching Ripon on the running in turn during the autumn of 1958.

The 'Bradford Express'

D49 No.62774 'The Staintondale' prepares to leave Bradford Forster Square with the 12.23 to Harrogate on Saturday 23 February 1957, the last day of this service. *(F. W. Smith)*

On 4 December 1876, the Midland Railway opened its line between Guiseley and Shipley. The North Eastern took the opportunity to negotiate running powers from Milnerwood Junction, on the Joint line west of Otley, into the Midland Station at Bradford (later Market Street and later still Forster Square).

A service of three trains each way began on 1 August 1877 leaving Harrogate at 8.40am, 12.05pm and 3.25pm and returning from Bradford at 10.25am, 2.00pm and 5.40pm. By 1880 there were four trains each way, all stopping at Otley, Guiseley and Shipley.

The entry in 'Bradshaw' for April 1910 is remarkable for its complicated conditional stops and footnotes. The '11th and 25th instant' were both Mondays, presumably market days. In 1922 there were similar stops at Pannal on alternate Mondays. One can only assume that the various request stops were the result of memorials from regular passengers whose journeys would be expedited if the 'Express' could be stopped at their local station.

The sort of customers who would have had sufficient influence to gain these concessions were probably those who subscribed to the club coach which ran between Harrogate and Bradford during the 1920s and 30s. It was attached to the 8.30am from Harrogate and 5.20pm from Bradford, both of which stopped only at Otley in the 1922 timetable,

HARROGATE and BRADFORD.—North Eastern.

Miles.	Week Days.	mrn	mrn	mrn	mrn	aft	aft	aft	aft	aft		
	Harrogate ....dep.	7 40	8 25	9 27	1130	1240	2 49	5 5	6 47	7 42	....	....
3¼	Pannal	....	....	....	....	....	....	n	....	....	....	....
6¾	Weeton	i	....	....	....	....	....	....	....	œ	....	....
12¾	Otley 718	8 3	8 45	9 47	1151	1 0	3 9	5 25	7 7	8 4	....	....
15¼	Menston	....	....	....	....	....	....	....	....	b	....	....
16¾	Guiseley	8 12	8 54	9 56	12 0	1 10	3 20	5 36	7 16	8 14	....	....
20	Baildon	....	....	....	....	....	....	v	....	....	....	....
21¼	Shipley † 610	8 21	9 3	10 5	12 9	1 19	3 33	5 47	7 25	8 23	....	....
23¾	Manningham ....[736, 788	b	b	b	b	b	b	b	b	b	....	....
24¾	Bradford (Market Street) 379,	8 30	9 12	1012	1218	1 28	3 40	5 55	7 33	8 30	....	....

Miles.	Week Days.	mrn	mrn	mrn	mrn	aft	aft	aft	aft	aft			
	Market Street Station, Bradford ....dep.	7 20	9 5	9 55	1118	1 13	3 20	5 27	6 8	8 55	....	....	....
1	Manningham	œ	œ	œ	œ	œ	œ	œ	œ	œ	....	....	....
2¾	Shipley †	7 27	9 14	10 3	....	1 20	3 27	5 34	6 17	9 0	....	....	....
4¼	Baildon	....	....	....	....	....	....	....	....	....	....	....	....
7½	Guiseley	7 38	9 24	1013	æ	1 31	3 36	5 43	6 29	9 10	....	....	....
9	Menston	....	....	l	....	....	....	....	....	....	....	....	....
11¾	Otley 718	7 50	9 32	1023	1138	1 40	3 45	5 51	6 39	9 18	....	....	....
17¾	Weeton	....	....	....	....	o	....	....	o	....	....	....	....
21	Pannal ....[714	8 5	....	n	....	h	nd	....	....	....	....	....	....
24¾	Harrogate 705, 708, arr.	8 14	9 51	1042	1158	2 3	4 8	6 12	7 1	9 43	....	....	....

b Set down if required from Harrogate and beyond.
d Stops if required to take up, and on Thursdays if required to set down.
h Stops if required to set down.
i Takes up if required for Otley and Bradford.
l Takes up if required for Harrogate and beyond.
n Stop if required on the 11th and 25th instant.
o Set down if required from Bradford, Manningham, or Otley.
v Sets down on Fridays if required from Newcastle.
æ Takes up for Harrogate on Saturdays.
œ Take up if required for Otley and beyond.
† Station Road: rather less than ½ mile from the G.N. (Bridge Street) Station.

☞ For **OTHER TRAINS** between Bradford and Otley, see pages 616 and 617.

completing the journey in 42 minutes. The coach was a six wheeled saloon with toilet, washroom and drinks cabinet. It was well appointed but given to rough riding. Only members were admitted. Arrival in Bradford was at 9.12am. There was an earlier 7.35 from Harrogate with more stops for ordinary commuters who had to be in their offices a little earlier than this.

To work the first train out of Bradford, the NER kept a single loco at the Midland Manningham shed. During the late 1920s it was class D23 No. 328.

Early in 1939, the LNER decided that traffic on certain Harrogate–Bradford trains was insufficient to justify 'normal train sets' yet too much for a Sentinel Car. They came to the same conclusion regarding the Pateley Bridge and Pilmoor branch trains.

As a compromise they created two push-pull formations, each comprising two carriages which were coupled semi permanently to class G5 locomotives: No. 387 based at Starbeck and No. 1839, the resident engine at Pateley Bridge.

The main financial saving was the wage of the guard who was not required on the push-pull. The Starbeck set was rostered to cover two 'off peak' trips to Bradford between two journeys to and from Pilmoor. When it was not available, a conventional train ran, usually also with a G5.

Wartime austerity brought a drastic reduction in the Harrogate to Bradford service and the cuts were never restored. In 1948 there were just two trains Mondays to Fridays leaving Harrogate at 8.25am and 3.35pm and Bradford at 10.35am and 5.15pm.

J39 No.64818 of Starbeck Shed at Menston with the 5.15p.m. Bradford Forster Square to Harrogate about 1952. *(F.W. Smith)*

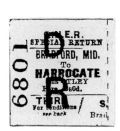

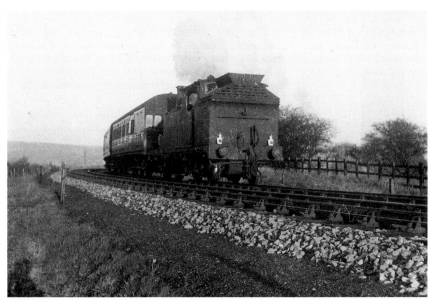

G5 0-4-4T No.67332 rounds the curve between Milnerwood and Menston Junctions with an afternoon Harrogate to Bradford train about 1949. *(F. W. Smith)*

There was a third train on a Saturday which left Harrogate at 10.50am in order to bring the commuters home on the 12.23 departure from Forster Square.

By 1950 there was only one train a day. The time honoured 8.25am now stopped at Pannal, Weeton, Pool, Otley, Guiseley and Shipley. It returned at 12.23 on Saturdays and 5.15pm Mondays to Fridays calling at the same stations plus Menston.

During the day, the Starbeck engine, usually a D49 'Hunt' did a trip from Bradford Forster Square to Leeds City and back. On both 19 and 21 December 1956, it got delayed in fog and missed its return working to Harrogate. Manningham Shed had to substitute a Stanier 2-6-2T which then also worked the final leg of the diagram, the 8.40pm Harrogate to Ripon. It took the empty carriages back to Harrogate and spent the night at Starbeck, returning to Bradford with the following morning's 8.25 from Harrogate.

When the service finished on Saturday 23 February 1957, the effect on through passengers was minimal. Since June 1954, Harrogate had enjoyed an hourly diesel service to Bradford Exchange. Trains did not negotiate the congested approach to Leeds City, which even then was bad. Instead they ascended the Gelderd curve into Leeds Central. After a quick reversal, they left via Holbeck High level passing over the busy tracks leading into Leeds City.

'Bradshaw' for April 1957 shows what is almost a direct replacement for the Forster Square train. Starting from Knaresborough, it left Harrogate at 8.20 for Weeton, Leeds Central, Stanningley and Bradford Exchange, arrive 9.07. The corresponding return was at 5.05pm from Bradford Exchange for Leeds Central, Weeton, Pannal, Harrogate, Starbeck and Knaresborough. This pair of trains continued into the early 1970s, even after the other through trains had been withdrawn.

The diesels even ran hourly on a Sunday. In summer they were extended to Knaresborough. In the one summer of 1960, there was also a Sundays only diesel service between Knaresborough, Harrogate and Bradford Forster Square via Otley.

From 1 May 1967, all traffic in Leeds was concentrated on City Station and Central was closed. This was much to the convenience of through passengers but the scheme was done on the cheap. Some previously segregated train movements now had to negotiate the same junctions.

During the summer of 1967, Harrogate to Bradford trains reversed at Leeds City but in September the two services were separated apart from the one peak hour through train.

Harrogate-Bradford today

Provided the trains run on time, the weekday journey can be accomplished every half hour in about 1 hour 7 minutes changing at Leeds. There is a choice of route to either Forster Square or Interchange, arrival times being almost simultaneous. Coming back, the wait in Leeds tends to be a little longer but Harrogate can be reached every half hour from either Bradford Station in about 1 1/4 hours. On Sundays the trains are less frequent and some of the waits in Leeds are slightly longer.

Today's journey is slower but more frequent than when there were through trains. But the 50 minute schedules of the 1954-67 period were via Leeds Central and were at the cost of leaving most intermediate stations with hardly any service at all.

Two of the original eight Derby Lightweight sets make up a four coach Knaresborough to Bradford Exchange working, seen between Wescoe Hill Tunnel and Weeton Station in the Summer of 1955.

(J. C. W. Halliday)

Pioneer Railcars

The streamlined Great Western cars were the only significant fleet of diesel railcars on British Railways prior to the appearance of the Derby Lightweights in 1954. No.20, on trial at Harrogate, on 24 August 1952, was built in 1940 and is preserved on the Kent & East Sussex Railway.

(H. Whitby/S. Askew Collection)

The traditional passenger train comprised a steam locomotive hauling one or more carriages. Especially on short journeys, the ritual of the engine running round at each terminus was such a pain that push-pull working was introduced on some routes. The next logical step was to try and combine the locomotive and passenger accommodation within the same vehicle. This concept found only limited application in steam days.

Nowadays, the entire fleet of Regional Railways North East comprises diesel and electric multiple units. So the changeover has not just been from steam to diesel and electric but also from locomotive to railcar or multiple unit working.

Harrogate was host to LNER steam and diesel railcars during the 1930s. In 1954 it received the first of what turned out to be a large fleet of BR diesel multiple units. Then in 1984 it saw an increase in its frequency of trains with the arrival of the first 'second generation' diesel vehicles.

The Sentinel Steam Railcars

A glance at 'Bradshaw' for April 1910 reveals a number of 'auto-car' workings on the Wetherby lines and between Harrogate and York. A North Eastern Railway 'auto-car' was not a railcar but a push-pull train with a 'BTP' 0-4-4 tank engine sometimes sandwiched between two driving trailers.

The first example of a steam railcar in the Harrogate area was the one bought by the Nidd Valley Light Railway in 1921 for use between Pateley Bridge and Lofthouse. Originally built for the Great Western Railway in 1905, it was named 'Hill' by its new owners who ran it until closure of the line to passengers in 1929. It had seats for 48 passengers and could be driven from either end. Photographs of 'Hill' appear in both Volumes One and Two of *Railways Around Harrogate*.

In 1927, the LNER tested a Sentinel steam railcar between York and Whitby. Photographs of the trial run appear in *Railways Around Whitby* (Volume One). By the mid 1930s they had 57 of these vehicles in the North Eastern area alone. At one end was a vertical steam boiler driving either a 2, 6, or 12 cylinder engine, the more powerful cars being designed for the more heavily graded routes. There was a driving compartment at both ends. The passenger saloon accommodated 60 people on tram type reversible seats. The engine compartment tended to get both hot and noisy. The driver could escape from this half the time when driving from the other end but the fireman was stuck with it. The cars first appeared in teak livery but later changed to green and cream. They tended to get very dirty because coal had to be dropped into the bunkers

hrough a door in the roof. Many carried names
eminiscent of old stage coaches.

In July 1932, there were two Sentinel cars
allocated to Starbeck: Nos 2268 'Emerald' and 2279
'Norfolk'. They worked half hourly from Harrogate
o Knaresborough and back, also occasionally to
Wetherby and Ripon. During the summer of 1939
they worked five return trips between Harrogate and
York.

On occasions they would work charter trains for
local clubs to the coast, Bridlington being a favourite
destination.

Other cars allocated to Starbeck during the 1930s
and early 40s were 2139 'Hark Forward', 2200
'Surprise' and 2257 'Defiance'. The last one to arrive
was No. 2147 'Woodpecker' which was transferred
from Neville Hill in October 1945 and withdrawn in
January 1947. It was replaced on the Harrogate to
Knaresborough service by a G5 push-pull set.

The Electric Autocars

The word autocar had also been used to describe
two petrol-electric vehicles built by the NER in May
1903. They had 52 seats mounted on two bogies
(i.e. they had eight wheels) and were powered by a
Napier engine driving a dynamo.

Teething problems delayed entry into service
until August 1904 when one car began running
between Scarborough and Filey, the other between
West Hartlepool and Hartlepool. From 1 July 1908
both cars worked the Selby to Cawood branch which
was their principal home on and off for most of their
lives.

From 1 July 1923, but only until the end of that
summer timetable, car No.3170 was based at
Starbeck working the following roster:

depart		arrive	miles
7.38	Starbeck to Harrogate (empty)	7.44	2¼
8.10	Harrogate to Ripon	8.27	11½
8.37	Ripon to Harrogate	8.57	11½
9.15	Harrogate to Wetherby	9.30	7¾
9.37	Wetherby to Harrogate	9.55	7¾
10.08	Harrogate to Pannal	10.15	3¼
10.20	Pannal to Harrogate	10.28	3¼
10.55	Harrogate to Pateley Bridge	11.32	14½
11.47	Pateley Bridge to Harrogate	12.24	14½
12.35	Harrogate to Wetherby	12.50	7¾
13.00	Wetherby to Harrogate	13.18	7¾
14.25	Harrogate to Pateley Bridge	15.02	14½
15.15	Pateley Bridge to Harrogate	15.52	14½
16.00	Harrogate to Pannal	16.07	3¼
16.20	Pannal to Harrogate	16.28	3¼
17.15	Harrogate to Knaresborough	17.25	4
17.45	Knaresborough to Harrogate	17.57	4
18.05	Harrogate to Starbeck (empty)	18.109	2¼
			137½

The two cars 3170 and 3171 were withdrawn in
1930/31 having latterly seen little use. The petrol-
electric technology was not pursued.

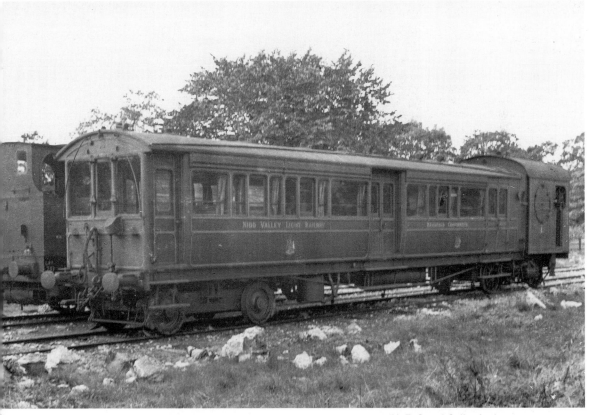

Railcar 'Hill' of the Nidd Valley Light Railway.   (N. E. Stead Collection)

The LNER diesel railcars

By the early 1930s, the diesel engine was proving a reliable source of propulsion for road lorries and buses and was being considered by the railway companies. In 1931/32, Armstrong Whitworth built for the LNER three 60 seat 250 horse power diesel – electric railcars. They were mounted on bogies – that is to say they were eight wheelers.

A photograph appears in Volume One showing No. 232 'Northumbrian' leaving York for Harrogate in August 1935 when it was based at Neville Hill covering similar duties to the Sentinel steam cars.

Prior to this, 'Northumbrian' had been fitted out as private saloon with luxurious accommodation for 12 passengers. For two weeks in February/March 1933, it ran as the 'Armstrong-Shell Express'

between London Euston and Castle Bromwich, near Birmingham achieving speeds of up to 70mph conveying guests of Armstrong Whitworth and Shell to the British Industries Fair. It was then converted back for ordinary use and purchased by the LNER.

The three diesel cars were withdrawn during 1939. They then languished at Darlington for at least five years before being scrapped.

The LMS experimented with diesel railcars on a similar modest scale. The Great Western Railway operated the only significant fleet in mainland Britain prior to the BR programme of 1954 onwards. There were diesel railcars in Ireland, notably those of the County Donegal Joint Committee.

A Sentinel steam railcar approaching Ripon about 1932.

(J. W. Hague/David Beeken Collection)

The experimental diesel multiple unit comprising three 4 wheel vehicles travelling south between Northallerton and Thirsk during trials in 1952.

(J. W. Hague/David Beeken Collection)

The Derby Lightweights

In the light of more recent experience, it may be of passing interest to recall the experimental diesel multiple unit which was afforded a trial on British Railways in the years 1952-54.

According to *Trains Illustrated* (July 1952), 'the basic principle is the application to a railway vehicle of selected features of bus and coach design added to the great advantage which a railway vehicle possesses in its much lower rolling resistance and the easier gradients which it uses'.

The subject of the trial was a train of three four wheel vehicles working in multiple, driven from either end.

In November 1952, it was announced that the first full scale diesel multiple unit scheme would be in Yorkshire 'where it is considered that new and frequent services will be most effective in improving rail services and developing travel' (*Trains Illustrated* January 1953).

Fortunately for passengers between Harrogate, Leeds and Bradford, BR did not subject them to a fleet of four wheelers before deciding that bogie vehicles were best. They discarded the four wheel concept at the experimental stage.

14 June 1954 saw the entry into service of eight twin car 'Derby Lightweight' units. Each set comprised a motor composite, numbered 79000 to 79007 and a motor brake third, 79500 to 79507. There was seating for 130 passengers: 16 in first class the rest in third. Purists found the new trains cramped compared to steam trains and took exception to vibration from underfloor engines. Others liked the better view especially that available from the forward saloon where one could sit behind the driver – in first class at one end but in third at the other. (It wasn't redesignated second class until 1956).

Because of the gradients, both carriages were powered with two 150 horse power Leyland engines. Later variants of the class included power car plus trailer formations.

The diesel trains ran half hourly from Bradford Exchange to Leeds Central with alternate trains continuing to Harrogate. Generally they missed most intermediate stations. There was a mid morning service through to Ripon. On summer Sundays they ran from Bradford to Knaresborough. They also provided stopping services between Bradford and Leeds via the Pudsey loop. Overall they operated about 60% more miles than the steam trains which they replaced. Over the next four years they increased revenue five fold. (*Trains Illustrated* January 1959).

The eight original Derby Lightweights lasted only until January 1964. Other members of the class were all withdrawn by 1969. Their short life was due both to mechanical defect and to problems with the bodywork. Two sets (not from the first series) found their eventual way in to preservation via the Derby Research Centre. The set preserved on the Great Eastern Railway is a diesel but the one on the East Lancashire Railway was converted to battery operation in 1958.

Despite their short lives, the eight pioneer Derby Lightweights held a significance in the development of British Railways which was to last for at least the next 45 years. All the dmu variants which emerged from various workshops over the next seven years were fundamentally the same concept, similar in both internal and external appearance.

Derby Lightweight unit No.79007/79507 passing Ripon empty on 19 October 1954 bound for the Newcastle area where it was to go on trial prior to diesel multiple units being introduced there.

(J. W. Hague)

79000/79500, the first of a long line of BR diesel multiple units makes a trial run on 21 May 1954. It is seen (above) in Starbeck Station and (below) crossing the Stray, south of Harrogate Station on its way back to Leeds.

(H. Whitby/S. Askey Collection)

The Calder Valley Sets

From New Years Day 1962, the hourly Harrogate – Leeds–Bradford diesel was incorporated into a new semi fast service to Manchester via the Calder Valley. Alternate trains continued to Liverpool. This was no task for a local dmu. The Derby Lightweights were shunted aside in favour of a fleet of 30 'Calder Valley' sets. Later designated class 110, these were the Rolls Royce of the dmu fleet, quite literally because that is where their four 180 horse power engines came from. They were also the last of the line. After 1961, BR acquired no further diesel multiple unit stock until 1984.

Each three coach set comprised a motor brake composite, a trailer second and a motor composite. In total there were 24 first class seats, 12 in the leading saloon at each end, plus 159 second class. Even the latter were fitted with high backs giving greater comfort and more privacy than the bus type seats on some of the more ordinary dmus.

The class 110s were the mainstay of the Calder Valley (Leeds–Bradford–Manchester) service until well into the 1980s. They also worked further afield and still visited Harrogate after the through service was withdrawn in 1967. Their final years were not very happy. Up until 1983, 28 sets remained, all well cared for at Hammerton Street Depot, near Bradford. The other two had been damaged in accidents.

In 1983, the centre trailer cars were removed from most sets taking with them 40% of the seating capacity. Then Hammerton Street was closed leaving the remaining high powered two car formations to work from a common pool at Neville Hill, Leeds rostered on an interchangeable basis with inferior units. The introduction of class 144 'pacers' put them out of their misery by 1988. A three car set is preserved on the East Lancashire Railway and a two car on the Lakeside & Haverthwaite.

A Harrogate to Manchester Victoria train worked by a class 110 'Calder Valley' dmu passing Arthington on 20 March 1965. *(D. J. Mitchell)*

When the class 141s entered service in 1984, they were painted in the then West Yorkshire PTE bus livery as a sop to the organisation which had sponsored them.
(Martin Bairstow)

The 141s

After 1962, so many local passenger trains were withdrawn that it became possible to eliminate steam traction without the need to build any more diesel multiple units.

By the early 1980s, most non-electric local and medium distance services were still operated by the same fleet of dmus which were all around 25 years old. There was no appetite for further closures but nor were there any plans for dmu replacement.

As the situation became more and more urgent, BR faced political pressure to come up with a solution which, above all, had to appear cheap. In 1981, they produced the experimental class 140, a pair of four wheel vehicles based as much as possible on bus technology. It was a repeat of the 1952 story except that this time they decided to go ahead with a production run of 20 similar units of class 141. They managed to sell the idea to the West Yorkshire PTE which agreed partly to finance the venture as the new trains would run both within and just outside their area.

Delivered in 1983/4, each two car unit had bus type seats for 94 people which was less than the trains they were to replace. The bodies were made from standard parts for a Leyland National bus making them narrower than conventional railway vehicles. Both carriages were powered so they had no problem with the local gradients. They tended to ride well on welded track but badly on rail joints.

The 20 trains entered full service with the May 1984 timetable. Amongst their rosters was the Leeds–Harrogate–York route which was doubled in frequency to half hourly between Leeds and Knaresborough.

Over subsequent years, frequencies were similarly increased on other routes coinciding with the introduction of new rolling stock. In this regard Harrogate was the first but the price for this was its being saddled with the class 141s. These were hardly a suitable complement to the longer distance trains from Leeds and York for which they were supposed to act as feeders.

The 141s were a deliberately inferior product designed to meet the political needs of the day. As events have turned out, they were a necessary evil in only to prove:

(1) That there is no point building a train to less than the permitted loading gauge. This point was rectified in the class 142, 143 and 144s which were built over the next four years.
(2) A four wheel vehicle is inferior to a bogie one, a defect rectified in the class 150 and later series which appeared from 1986.
(3) Railway passengers expect something better than bus seats (and to judge by many recent new buses, so do bus passengers).

By the early 1990s, most neighbouring lines were in the hands of class 155, 156 and 158 'supersprinters'. Harrogate retained 141s until September 1995 when electrification in Airedale and Wharfedale permitted transfer of mainly three car 144 sets. These are of full size but are still four wheelers with bus seats.

All the 141s were withdrawn by mid 1998. At the time of writing, the majority are laid up at Doncaster awaiting their fate.

141113 pauses at Weeton with a York-Harrogate-Leeds service.

(Martin Bairstow)

Not quite up to Pullman standard, passengers endure a class 141 as it bounces its way from Leeds to Harrogate in 1985. *(Martin Bairstow)*

Ten out of the 28 class 144s are three car sets. 144021 calls at Headingley in 1991. *(Martin Bairstow)*

Camping Coaches

In June 1933, the LNER carried out a rapid conversion of ten redundant carriages in order to make them available from 1 July as camping coaches. The experiment was judged a success so the following year they converted another 25. Not only that but the idea was copied by the LMS and Great Western Railways in 1934 with the Southern joining in 1935. By the outbreak of War in 1939 there were over 400 camping coaches available for hire at numerous locations throughout the country.

The accompanying photograph shows one of the original ten coaches in 1933. It is standing in a siding about half a mile north west of Pateley Bridge station alongside the track which used to connect the NER to the Nidd Valley Light Railway. Just off the right of the picture, there is a weir which explains why the river is so wide and deep at this point.

To the left of the carriage, above the lady on the diving board, can be seen the course of the rope worked incline which used to like the Scot Gate Ash Quarry to the NER goods yard. Built in the 1870s, this closed during the First World War. On the extreme right of the photo is the station building of the Nidd Valley Light Railway which, at that time, had been closed to passengers and general freight but remained open for the reservoir construction traffic.

The camping coach is still in teak livery. It carries its original number and still sports large numerals on each compartment door denoting third class. The green and cream livery was not introduced until 1935. No. 42345 was an ex Great Northern six wheeler dating from 1887. Of the five compartments, one has been converted into a kitchen, two combined to make a living room and two have become bedrooms. There was no internal access between the living room and the sleeping accommodation. Toilet facilities were normally available at the station but at Pateley Bridge this was half a mile away so there must have been some local arrangement.

For the second season, 1934, the LNER advertised that a camping coach was available on the Pateley Bridge branch and could be hired at any station, Forge Valley, Birstwith, Darley, Dacre or Pateley Bridge at the patrons' option.

From 1937, they offered four coaches on the branch. These were permanently based at Forge Valley, Dacre and two at Pateley Bridge.

On page 41 of *Railways Around Whitby Volume Two* there is a photograph of the Touring Camping Coach. This was a former sleeping car built by the NER in 1905.

It was converted to a camping coach in 1935 and offered parties of six or seven people a week long holiday starting from York on a Saturday. It spent three nights at Pateley Bridge 'for boating, river bathing and splendid rambling country', two nights at Aysgarth and two at Glaisdale. It travelled attached to ordinary passenger trains. (Not with the pick up goods as stated in error in *Railways Around Whitby Volume Two*).

The camping coach facility was withdrawn at the start of the Second World War and the carriages put to other uses. By the time the service was relaunched in 1952, the Pateley Bridge line was closed to passenger traffic so the coaches never returned.

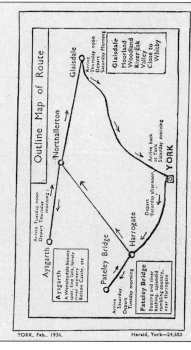

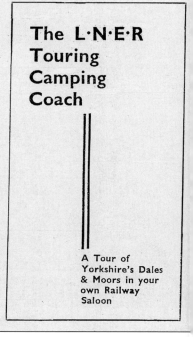

Taking the plunge at Pateley Bridge in 1933.

Wayside Stations

The four stations between Harrogate and York which closed in September 1958 were all at remote locations. Latterly very few trains had stopped. Hessay, for example, only had a 7.27am to Harrogate and a 8.00am to York plus an extra each way on Saturdays.

Today the rural station lives on at Cattal, Hammerton and Poppleton, each of which now enjoys an hourly service. They are unstaffed for retail purposes but each retains a signalman who carries out the time honoured rituals of opening the crossing gates, pulling off the semaphore signals and collecting the single line token.

Some of the wayside stations on closed lines were extremely ill served. Immediately before closure, Ripley Valley had just one train in the Harrogate direction only, In 1956, Sinderby had one train, southbound only at 7.24am. Pickhill was served by this same train plus one at 8.51pm, again southbound only. At the same period, Nidd Bridge had four trains southbound, but only one toward Ripon, Wormald Green had three and one respectively. In some cases the purpose of an unbalanced early morning call was the unloading of mail and parcels.

Between Harrogate and Leeds, two stations have disappeared: The two level interchange at Holbeck was virtually redundant by the time of closure in 1958. The remote junction station at Arthington closed with the Otley branch in 1965.

Sinderby looking north in 1962. Closed at the end of 1961, the station had, in its last few years, been served by just one train per day, southbound only at 7.08a.m. from Northallerton to Leeds City.
(Stations UK)

Wilstrop Siding, one mile east of Hammerton, was served Saturdays only by the 11a.m. train from Harrogate and the 3.22p.m. back from York. Its sole purpose was to allow railway and other local families to go shopping once a week. *(Stations UK)*

A class 104 four car dmu passing the closed station at Goldsborough, bound for Harrogate in July 1959.
(Peter Sunderland)

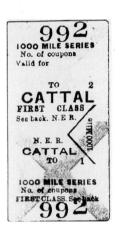

Above:
Cattal Station looking towards Harrogate in 1984.
(Martin Bairstow)

Right:
Poppleton also retains a manual signal box with hand operated gates. Just on the Harrogate side of the station is the nursery which supplies landscaping, hanging baskets etc. for stations in the area. It is served by a 2 foot gauge line worked by an 0-4-0 diesel dating from 1940 called 'Alne'.
(Martin Bairstow)

40148 leaving Pool in Wharfedale for Leeds on 3 January 1959. By that time this station only saw two trains one way and three the other. *(P. B. Booth/N. E. Stead Collection)*

80120 passing Pannal with the 11.50a.m. Harrogate to Kings Cross on 25 March 1961. At that time Pannal had long intervals between stopping trains but now has a half hourly frequency.

(D. Butterfield/N. E. Stead Collection)

Hampsthwaite Station opened four years after the branch line and closed at the end of 1949, fifteen months before the withdrawal of passenger services to Pateley Bridge.

(F. W. Smith Collection)

Arthington on its final day, 22 March 1965. A Harrogate to Leeds dmu passes through non stop.

(F. W. Smith Collection)

4116 calls at Burley Park on 0 May 1992.

(Martin Bairstow)

Forgotten Junctions

Starbeck North in 1972 after abandonment of the route to Bilton Junction. This track bed can be walked or cycled from here to the south end of Bilton Viaduct.

(M. A. King)

Melmerby looking towards Northallerton about 1966. The abandoned Thirsk line is to the right. That to Masham is on the left.

(F. W. Smith Collection)

Crimple Junction looking towards Harrogate after closure of the Wetherby branch. The line from Pannal curves in before the viaduct.

(F. W. Smith Collection)

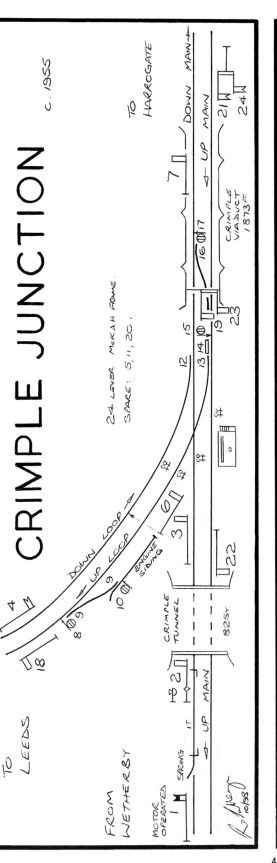

CRIMPLE JUNCTION

c. 1955

TO HARROGATE

24 LEVER McKAH FRAME.
SPARE: 5, 11, 20.

CRIMPLE VIADUCT 1873ft.

CRIMPLE TUNNEL

82 Sy.

TO LEEDS

FROM WETHERBY

MOTOR OPERATED

SPRING

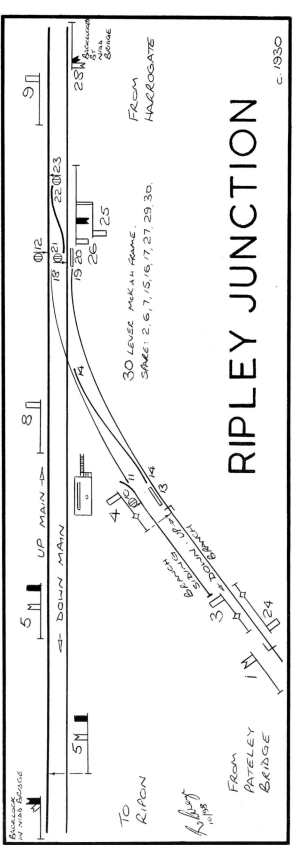

RIPLEY JUNCTION

c. 1930

FROM HARROGATE

BACKLOCK BY NIDD BRIDGE

30 LEVER McKAH FRAME.
SPARE: 2, 6, 7, 15, 16, 17, 27, 29, 30.

UP MAIN

DOWN MAIN

DOWN BRANCH

BRANCH SIDING

FROM PATELEY BRIDGE

TO RIPON

BACKLOCK IN NIDD BRIDGE

47

Penda's Way

By E. P. Barrington

On 5 June 1939, the LNER opened an additional station at Penda's Way to serve a large new housing estate. The name recalls the battle nearby in 654 when King Penda of Mercia was slain. According to Trains Illustrated (February 1961), "the two 120 yard long wooden platforms (electrically lit compared to the more usual gas at the other stations) are reported to have been built in a day". Ted Barrington confirms this because he saw it happen.

I was only five years old at the time but I can remember the station suddenly appearing complete with footbridge on the weekend prior to the opening date. My home was at what was No. 116 (now 140) Penda's Way about eight houses away from the station entrance. We had a long back garden and, in wartime, an allotment along the top of the banking.

As youngsters we used to play around the four concrete pillars supporting the station footbridge or, if we could make it without being seen, underneath the ramp at the northern end of the platform. We had to take care when a northbound train stopped in case we got scalded or covered in steam.

I travelled on the 1.31 pm Sentinel car to Cross Gates. We called them 'steam pigs'. Amongst those used on the branch were 'Hope', 'Hark Forward', 'Integrity', 'Woodpecker', 'Criterion' and 'Recovery'. Occasionally they worked duties besides those shown as third class only in the timetable.

I had the unusual experience of travelling to Leeds on the 8.58 am behind 6401 'James Fitzjames' whilst it was on loan to the area. This was the train which started from Leeds to Church Fenton then went forward to Wetherby and back to Leeds.

The two ex LBSCR 4-4-0s, 2051 and 2068 were noted twice as freight pilots on the branch. An unidentified 'King Arthur' passed very late one night working southbound alone on a freight.

My favourite locos on this line were the D20s, such a pity that one was not saved for posterity after such faithful service. I also liked the five class V1s, 415-7, 454 and 455, brought from the North East to inaugurate the heavy trains used to get workers to the Royal Ordnance Factory at Thorp Arch.

At the end of the War, we had permission to hold our VE day celebrations for the estate in the northbound waiting room. Mrs Harding was then the porter. She had been preceded by a porter named George who lived near the Station Hotel at Cross Gates and was followed by Ted Watson with whom I became very friendly in later years spending many a happy hour talking and keeping warm in the booking office helping with the ticket returns and topping up the fire buckets outside the staff toilet at the opposite end of the waiting room to the ticket office.

80118 restarts its Harrogate to Leeds train from Penda's Way in June 1959. The rear coach is an empty Pullman car. This photo was taken a few moments after the one referred to in the text opposite.

(Peter Sunderland)

During the War freight trains sometimes ran into trouble coming up the bank between Cross Gates and Penda's Way especially if they had been stopped by signals in Cross Gates Station. Some of the culprits were USA Transportation Corps 2-8-0s running through to the North East. On one occasion a train had struggled up the bank until the loco reached the platform where it expired. One of the wagons was smouldering and I ran to the station to tell the crew but they already knew and were lashing with buckets to deal with the outbreak. Later the same day I was told that this wagon held bombs. Who knows, we may have had another Soham disaster if it hadn't been noticed quickly enough.

A slightly later memory is of J21 No. 65036 returning from Darlington resplendent in a new coat of paint and BRITISH RAILWAYS on the tender. Within a short time the tender was exchanged for a grubby one and in only a few weeks 65036 was withdrawn.

On another occasion a southbound double headed freight had J20 64690 as pilot. It stood at the signals quite a while before wending its way down to Neville Hill. I never saw it return so it presumably made its way back to its home territory by a different route. I noted many new locos on the test train which returned to Darlington via the Wetherby branch about 4pm each weekday. On one occasion it passed No. 61600 'Sandringham' ex works going towards Leeds. In later years the Newcastle to Llandudno Saturday trains created possibly the most interest. (A photograph appears in volume one of class A4 No. 60032 'Gannet' on this working).

Quite often, going to work, I used to leave home at 8.08 for the 8.09 train to Leeds dashing onto the embankment, along the edge of the allotments and down to the foot crossing at the south end of the station. One morning as I darted across the track, I realised that the approaching train wasn't stopping. It was a troop train and it just missed me. After that I left home a little bit earlier and used the official route.

Peter Sunderland's photo on page 52 of volume one showing a standard 2-6-4T (I believe No. 80118) was taken near the top of our garden. The four figures on the platform are my parents, myself and porter Ted Watson.

Let us hope that West Yorkshire PTE's long term aim to reopen at least part of this line will come to fruition bringing frequent trains back to Penda's Way.

The 5.35p.m. Leeds City to Harrogate dmu calls at Bardsey in June 1963. Dieselisation did not improve the service to stations on the Wetherby line. *(J. M. Rayner)*

0067 · 2nd · SPECIAL CHEAP SINGLE · SPECIAL CHEAP SINGLE · 2nd · 0067
Thorner to
Thorner Scholes / Thorner Scholes
SCHOLES
(N) (N)
For conditions see over · For conditions see over

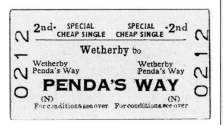

0212 · 2nd · SPECIAL CHEAP SINGLE · SPECIAL CHEAP SINGLE · 2nd · 0212
Wetherby to
Wetherby Penda's Way / Wetherby Penda's Way
PENDA'S WAY
(N) (N)
For conditions see over · For conditions see over

2244 · 3rd · SPECIAL CHEAP DAY · SPECIAL CHEAP DAY · 3rd · 2244
CHILD
Leeds (City) to PENDA'S WAY / Pendas Way TO LEEDS (CITY)
Fare 0/5 · Fare 0/5
For conditions see over · For conditions see over

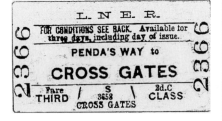

2366 · L. N. E. R. · 2366
FOR CONDITIONS SEE BACK. Available for three days, including day of issue.
PENDA'S WAY to
CROSS GATES
Fare / S / 2d.C
THIRD 3658 CROSS GATES CLASS

2nd · SPECIAL SINGLE · SPECIAL SINGLE · 2nd
1086 · 1086
Thorner to
Thorner Penda's Way / Thorner Penda's Way
PENDA'S WAY
(N) 0/5 FARE 0/5 (N)
For conditions see over · For conditions see over

3rd · SPECIAL CHEAP DAY · SPECIAL CHEAP DAY · 3rd
0126 · 0126
D
Osmondthorpe to PENDA'S WAY / Penda's Way TO OSMONDTHORPE
(N) Fare 0/7 · Fare 0/7 (N)
For conditions see over · For conditions see over

LNER

CHEAP FARES
BETWEEN
PENDA'S WAY
AND LEEDS

5d Third Day Single
8d Third Return
Return halves available
three months

THIRD CLASS SEASON TICKET

	£ s. d.
1 week	3 6
1 month	14 0
3 months	2 0 0
6 months	4 0 0
12 months	7 15 0

First Class Fares 50% more
WORKMEN'S TICKETS
6½d DAILY
3/3 WEEKLY
(For particulars of trains by which Workmen's Tickets are available see separate bill)

May 1939 · T P W Ltd—1250

LNER

TRAVEL
BY RAIL
BETWEEN
Penda's Way
and Leeds
CHEAP FARES
and TRAIN SERVICE
5th JUNE to 23rd SEPT 1939

Carry this card in your wallet or handbag

TRAIN SERVICE 5th June to 23rd Sept. 1939.
WEEKDAYS ONLY

To LEEDS		To PENDA'S WAY	
PENDA'S WAY depart	LEEDS (City) arrive	LEEDS (City) depart	PENDA'S WAY arrive
am	am	am	am
7 30	7 45	6 34	6 50
8 10	8 24	7 56	8 12
8 41	8 53	9 50	10 6
8 58	9 13	pm	pm
pm	pm	†12 12	12 27
12 58	1 13	1 0 SO	1 14
1 13 SO	1 24	1 28	1 44
*1 31 SX	1 44	4 32	4 48
2 3 SO	2 12	5 35	5 51
2 29	2 44	6 5 SX	6 21
5 7	5 20	6 35	6 51
5 44	5 59	7 15	7 31
6A42	6 55	8 50	9 6
7 44	7 59	*9 55	10 11
9 39	9 54	11 0 WFSO	11 14

SO—Saturdays only
SX—Saturdays excepted
*—One Class only
A—Saturdays excepted until 1st July, daily after that date

WFSO—Wednesdays, Fridays and Saturdays only
†—One Class only SX

IT'S QUICKER BY RAIL

A Lost Commuter Route?

The 4.19p.m. Leeds City to Thorp Arch at Wetherby on 23 May 1958 behind D49 No.62740 'The Bedale'.
(M. Mitchell)

It was not uncommon for Conservative MPs to defend their having supported the 'general findings' of the Beeching Report whilst arguing that threatened services in their own constituencies should be viewed as special cases. The member for Scarborough & Whitby explained that he would have carried less weight in the latter quest if he had declared himself a rebel in the division lobby. The member for Bury took the theme a step further. Opposing the 1964 threatened closure of the Manchester to Bury electric lines, he defended having voted in favour of the Beeching Report because 'otherwise trains would still be running to Wetherby'.

One explanation for this seemingly odd remark (to a Lancashire audience) may have been that the honourable member hailed from Wetherby. In addition, Wetherby had earned the distinction in January 1964 of being the first closure implemented under the Beeching Report – as opposed to those which were already in the pipeline prior to publication.

What had the Wetherby line done to deserve this accolade?

At the time of closure, Wetherby Station itself saw an average of just 30 passengers a day. It had 14 staff and was able to display nine best kept station certificates. Some of the other branch stations will have performed even worse. Tadcaster, Newton

Kyme and Thorp Arch probably saw no passengers at all, given that they were served in one direction only by an early morning train which made a circuit from Leeds City via Garforth, Church Fenton, Wetherby and back to Leeds. Its sole traffic between Church Fenton and Wetherby must have been parcels to Tadcaster.

Between Leeds and Wetherby there were four trains, just one of which went through to Harrogate. In the other direction there were six. Four of these were clustered in the morning peak, one at lunchtime and one later afternoon. Two started from Harrogate and one came via Church Fenton. Except on Saturdays, it was impossible to get from Wetherby to Harrogate and back the same day.

The service at closure was more or less that reproduced in *Volume One* for Winter 1960-61 except that the morning Leeds-Tadcaster train had been withdrawn beyond Wetherby. It was a shadow of the 1932 timetable reproduced on the same page of *Volume One*.

Diesel multiple units had taken over the workings in January 1959 but, in contrast to some neighbouring lines, their arrival had not brought an improved frequency of trains. In an area quite liberally supplied with buses and at a time of rapidly rising car ownership, the train service was a bit of a joke.

Other traffic over the Wetherby lines was also much diminished. There were a few passenger trains non-stop between Leeds and Harrogate which had been diverted via Wetherby in recent years. This was partly because of shorter signal box opening hours since 1959 on the Arthington route and partly to avoid reversal at Leeds City for certain Liverpool-Newcastle expresses. Most through freight had been diverted away from Wetherby in 1959 following the completion of four tracks on the East Coast Main Line between Northallerton and York. This had allowed closure of the direct Wetherby West to East curve in the autumn of 1960. Traffic to the Thorp Arch Circular Railway had also ceased in 1958.

There remained some excursion traffic both out and inbound. The leaflet reproduced on the inside back cover shows a typical day excursion to Scarborough. Note the stop on the return journey only at Stutton station which had closed to normal traffic in 1905 and where only one platform survived.

On Wetherby race days the railway still came to life but excursion traffic was amongst that which Dr Beeching was most keen to ditch. He didn't like resources in reserve for occasional use only.

So with Dr Beeching complaining at the delay in implementing his Report, the Wetherby lines must have seemed an ideal candidate to rush through the consultative machinery. The Minister of Transport decreed that hardship to users would be minimal and the passenger service ended on Saturday 4 January 1964, that was within $9^{1}/_{2}$ months of the Beeching Report appearing in print.

The closure merited only a tiny mention in the *Yorkshire Post* whose leader column the same day was more concerned with the trial of new staff uniforms at Huddersfield Station. Apparently critics could not decide whether they made railwaymen look like General De Gaulle or like Nazi officers. (One assumes that such commentators had never met either). The editorial concluded that Dr Beeching would need more than new uniforms to get passengers on to his trains. It suggested that he might try leaving some lines open. This last comment was a general remark not linked to the first post Beeching closure so briefly recorded on another page but whose significance was not noticed. The press and public already knew Dr Beeching as the 'axeman' but few people had detailed knowledge of what was actually taking place.

On 4 January, the 5.35pm dmu from Leeds City to Harrogate carried a wreath from a customer 'in affectionate memory of 18 years of safe travel from Collingham Bridge'. Thus began the dismembering of about half the country's railway mileage. The through passenger trains were re-routed from the following Monday leaving the line open only for a short time until the local pick-up goods was withdrawn. Then began the ritual of lifting the track followed by piecemeal disposal of the right of way.

A leading reference work on the Wetherby lines is the article in *Trains Illustrated*, February 1961 by D.

Bertram. This prompted correspondence in the April issue including a letter from Mr A. E. W. Gregson of Thorner from which I would like to quote. 37 years later, some of the comments may appear dated but the general thrust shows a great deal of foresight.

I would like to dispute his easy dismissal of the Wetherby-Cross Gates branch. Its stations all serve villages which are growing dormitory areas for the city of Leeds and, despite the fairly frequent bus services it is just not true that the railway line is a slower and more indirect route.

Journey times to Leeds (in minutes)

	Bus	Train
Scholes	22	13
Thorner	25	19
Bardsey	25	24
Collingham Bridge	36	29
Wetherby	42	35

The few diesel trains still serving the area contrast sharply in comfort with the bone-jarring, swaying buses which navigate the narrow country roads forming the major part of their route mileage. I am sure that the railways could attract a profitable amount of passenger traffic on this branch provided that they gave a sufficiently frequent service. The present service is in a local phrase, 'neither nowt nor summat', and with the last departure of the day at 5.35pm from Leeds is quite useless to anyone working in that city. An hourly interval service during the day, increased to every 20 minutes at rush hours would be quite a different proposition, especially if it were continued up to 11pm. Moreover, all the stations on the branch have useful space in which cars might be parked. If this were offered as a free facility, it might tempt many who now journey by road to Leeds, for the parking problem in that city grows more difficult day by day.

Judged by the standards of the time, the sacrifice of the Wetherby branch was a pure formality. The meagre service and poor patronage were an irrelevance to local needs. But could the Leeds to Wetherby branch have had some potential?

It is unfortunate that Wetherby did not gain more from dieselisation in 1959. Contrast Ilkley where the diesels did bring a regular interval service. This helped maintain sufficient support to mount a credible case against closure. In the event Ilkley survived, under constant threat for at least ten years, until it was finally adopted into the PTE network. Now it has four electric trains departing every hour and the service does continue until after 11pm.

Today there would certainly be more than 30 passengers a day using Wetherby Station. Based on what has happened on other lines, it is fair to assume that trains to Leeds would be half hourly. There would be free car parks at each station and there might be a substantial park and ride facility where the line went under the A64 York Road north of Scholes.

Since the mid 1980s, long term plans of the West Yorkshire PTE have included rebuilding the

Through traffic such as this Saturday 11.30 Manchester Exchange to Newcastle express could always be rerouted via Arthington or York. V2 No.60878 nears the summit of the Cross Gates to Wetherby line at Whinmoor on 11 August 1962.

(M. Mitchell)

From January 1961 until January 1964, diesel hauled Trans Pennine expresses via Harrogate preferred the Wetherby route because it avoided reversal in Leeds. D183 (46046) has the 11a.m. Liverpool-Newcastle just past Spofforth on 19 October 1963.

(M. Mitchell)

Bardsey is rather less of a sparse rural community than when this postcard was taken in the 1920s. The main road bottom right is also a bit busier.

(Peter E. Baughan Collection)

Wetherby branch from Cross Gates as far as Scholes or possibly to a park and ride station by the A64. The scheme is supported by Leeds City Council whose Unitary Development Plan protects the abandoned route as far as Scholes Station though not, apparently, the short stretch thence to the A64.

Unfortunately, during the past 12 years or so, the PTE has been unable to progress even the much simpler reopening between Halifax and Huddersfield where the track is in situ.

Against this background it is going to be so long before the Scholes project could go ahead that one fears the PTE giving up hope and letting the Council grant planning consent to block the route. If this were to happen, it would be short term thinking in the extreme because, sooner rather than later, the authorities are going to have to face up to the problems of congestion and pollution.

Looking beyond Scholes and the A64, the railway has been redeveloped in places particularly with houses on the station sites at Thorner, Bardsey and Collingham Bridge thought not Wetherby which is just a car park. These obstacles need not be unsurmountable. A future railway would not be laid out for steam locomotives. One possibility for the Scholes to Wetherby route might be as an extension of the long proposed Leeds 'supertram' whose articulated rolling stock could tackle the gradients and curves necessary to forge alternative alignments without threatening properties built on the old one.

The remaining unencroached sections ought to be protected.

The station house at Collingham Bridge forms part of a new estate. Behind the camera, a new side street is named Dewar Close in honour of the last full time station master.

(Martin Bairstow)

Waiting for the rails to be relaid? The track bed between Penda's Way and Scholes.

(Martin Bairstow)

An excursion to Bridlington arriving at Collingham Bridge on a wet Whit Sunday in 1957 behind class B16 No.61428. There were normally no trains on a Sunday so Station Master Dewar would have had to open up specially.
(M. Mitchell)

J39 64934 climbs towards Thorner with a branch goods on 22 April 1960.
(M. Mitchell)

Class WD 2-8-0 No.90532 passing north through Thorner with a train of crippled wagons, probably destined for repair at Shildon. *(M. Mitchell)*

Standard 2-6-4T No.80116 calls at Bardsey with the 6p.m. Harrogate to Leeds City in May 1959.
(Peter Sunderland)

Wetherby Race Traffic

It was on race days that the Wetherby lines really came to life. From 1924 until 1959 there was a station at the racecourse itself.

After this closed, race specials still ran to Wetherby Station from where a bus link was provided to the racecourse. Trains came from Bradford, Sheffield, Doncaster and Hull but the most intensive operation was from Leeds.

After arrival at Wetherby trains moved on to stabling sidings at Collingham Bridge and Thorp Arch. Locos were turned on Wetherby triangle until that ceased to be available when the West to East curve was closed in 1960. That curve could also be used as a stabling facility. Sometimes an early arrival from Leeds would continue empty back to Leeds via Church Fenton in order to take up a second duty. This process could be reversed for the return service later in the day.

The operation brought out a variety of motive power including goods engines at the head of up to 12 non-corridor coaches. It also provided photographic opportunities. Mike Mitchell covered the Race Specials between 1957 and 1963. He was in action on Whit Monday 1959, the day when Peter Sunderland accompanied his friend Kenneth Field who had been commissioned by Ian Allan Ltd. to obtain photographs of the traffic – a mission which was partly frustrated by the 1959 strike in the printing industry.

The photographic feature which follows shows race traffic approaching Wetherby from all three directions. There is coverage of the empty stock movements necessary to store the carriages. Finally we follow the lucky or disappointed punters on their way home.

1963 was the final season for Wetherby Race trains because the line closed on the first weekend of 1964. Even without this final act, it is still likely that the traffic would have faded away quite soon. There would not have been the spare locomotives and rolling stock nor the siding space to store them. Demand for the trains would have fallen as more racegoers acquired their own cars. If one could somehow imagine a present day passenger service from Leeds to Wetherby of the type discussed in the previous chapter, then it is likely that there would be some extra race day business by ordinary train but no special provision for it.

Race Specials passing Scholes

EASTER MONDAY 7 APRIL 1958
(Noted by Mike Mitchell)

Time	Loco	No.	From
10.40	J39	64935	LEEDS CITY
11.00	J39	64835	LEEDS CITY
11.15	J39	64863	LEEDS CITY
11.37	J39	64922	LEEDS CITY
12.15	CRAB	42838	HUDDERSFIELD
12.25	J39	64730	LEEDS CITY
12.27	J39	64835	Returning empty to Leeds
12.40	8F	48652	DEWSBURY
13.00	J39	64725	LEEDS CITY

The J39 hauled trains would comprise non-corridor Gresley articulated coaches.

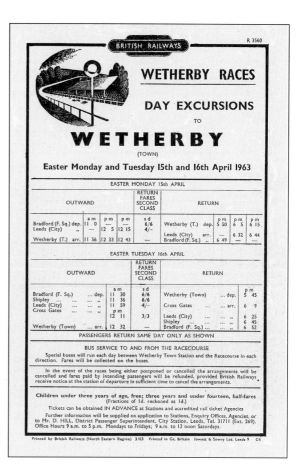

Departure of Trains after the Races

EASTER TUESDAY 3 APRIL 1956

Wetherby Racecourse Station (special trains)

PM	
5.05	Cross Gates, Leeds City
5.15	Harrogate, Otley, Guiseley, Shipley, Bradford Forster Square
5.25	Cross Gates, Leeds City
5.50	Church Fenton, Pontefract Baghill, Moorthorpe & South Kirby, Bolton on Dearne, Swinton Central, Kilnhurst Central, Parkgate & Aldwarke, Rotherham Central, Sheffield Victoria.

Wetherby Station (ordinary trains)

4.55	Collingham Bridge, Bardsey, Thorner, Scholes, Penda's Way, Cross Gates, Osmondthorpe, Marsh Lane, Leeds City.
6.16	Spofforth, Harrogate.

Wetherby Race Course Station looking towards Church Fenton. *(Stations UK)*

'Crab' 2-6-0 No.42789 approaching Bardsey with a Bradford Forster Square to Wetherby race special on Easter Tuesday 1963. *(J. M. Rayner)*

4986 attacks the difficult greasy cutting between Cross Gates and Penda's Way with a Bradford Forster Square to Wetherby race special on Easter Monday 1963. A following class 31 diesel hauled train from Sheffield had to be hand sanded up this section. *(M. Mitchell)*

39 64922 storms through Scholes with a Leeds-Wetherby special on Easter Monday 1958. There were six other similar Leeds-Wetherby workings that morning. *(M. Mitchell)*

The rare sight of a WD wi**
express passenger headcoc
(lamps over each buffe**
90127 coasts throug**
Collingham Bridge with **
Leeds-Wetherby special o**
Easter Monday 1961.
*(M. Mitche**

Specials from Bradford Forster Square sometimes came via Otley and Harrogate. 44965 passes the former Wetherby West Junction on the morning of Whit Monday 3 June 1963. The course of the by then abandoned West to East curve can be seen to the right of the engine.

(M. Mitchell)

Trains bringing punters fror** Sheffield could be routed vi** Church Fenton. B1 No.6100** 'Hartebeeste' approache** Newton Kyme on 10 Jun** 1957. *(M. Mitchel**

39 64870 has brought its nine coaches from Leeds into Wetherby Station in May 1959. *(Peter Sunderland)*

Meanwhile sister engine 64866 of Starbeck Shed is held in the cutting leading from the West Junction with its special from Bradford Forster Square via Harrogate.

(Peter Sunderland)

4870 now draws its stock out of the Station taking the east curve. *(Peter Sunderland)*

61

Next 4F No.44070 arrives from Sheffield via Church Fenton. We are now a short distance along the curve looking towards East Junction. *(Peter Sunderland)*

At last 64866 can now enter the station with its train from Bradford. *(Peter Sunderland)*

Once customers have alighted, it is propelled out along the Church Fenton line. *(Peter Sunderland)*

64863 has arrived with another excursion from Leeds. *(Peter Sunderland)*

It has taken its train forward to the site of the pre 1902 passenger station (just beyond East Junction). It has turned on the triangle and is now drawing forward 'wrong line' to its stabling point on the 'top side' of the triangle between east and west junctions. *(Peter Sunderland)*

44070 has taken its Sheffield excursion empty to Collingham Bridge where Station Master Dewar is waiting to supervise operations. The carriages will be shunted into the down siding behind the platform on the left. *(M. Mitchell)*

The engine will then go back to Wetherby for water and to turn on the triangle.
(Peter Sunderland)

Later, as the punters return to Wetherby Station, 44070, now facing the other way, draws its train out of the siding at Collingham Bridge and proceeds empty to pick up the Sheffield contingent.
(Peter Sunderland)

Its last sighting that day is at the approach to Stutton level crossing as it 'races' back to Sheffield Midland.
(Peter Sunderland)

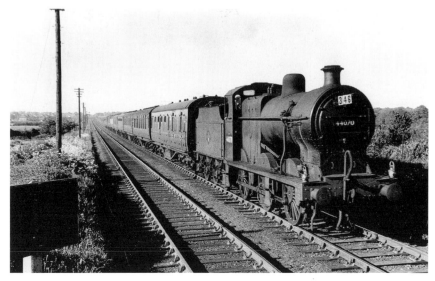

64863, which stabled on the top side of Wetherby triangle, must have set back to the old station then crossed over and drawn forward along the east to south curve to pick up its passengers. Here it is passing Collingham Bridge where Mr Dewar appears to manage a well kept station. He probably has time on most other days. *(M. Mitchell)*

80117 tackles the twisting gradients between Bardsey and Thorner with ten compartment coaches returning to Leeds on the evening of 3 June 1963. This was the last steam hauled Wetherby race special.

(M. Mitchell)

64944 threads the deep fireclay cutting on the approach to Thorner with a returning special for Leeds on 23 April 1962. The loco is running tender first because turning facilities at Wetherby had been lost the previous autumn with the severing of the West to East Junction section. *(M. Mitchell)*

J39 64947 assists Ivatt 2-6-0 No. 43161 through Thorner with a returning special to Sheffield on Whit Monday, 22 May 1961. *(M. Mitchell)*

B16 No.61415 at the head of a returning Leeds special on 19 April 1960. *(M. Mitchell)*

Before the decline set in, Collingham Bridge on the afternoon of Easter Monday 1957. On the right the crew of 64850 guard their heretegenous rake of coaches. A more modern set is stored in the left hand siding whilst further J39s occupy the running lines with light engine and empty stock movements.

(M. Mitchell)

Five years later, on 23 April 1962, the South to East Junction line is being used for storage. *(M. Mitchell)*

The Thorp Arch Circular Railway
by Richard D. Pulleyn

n Ivatt 2-6-0 at Walton Station with a workmen's train in July 1958.   (J. C. W. Halliday)

Many visitors to the Thorp Arch Industrial Estate, the Thorp Arch Shopping Centre, the British Library (or even Thorp Arch Prison!), may have wondered how much a large collection of buildings came to be built so far out in the country between Wetherby and York. The answer goes back to the Second World War when a suitable site was required for a new Royal Ordnance Factory, principally to manufacture bombs. Clearly such work was hazardous in the extreme, so the factory had to be constructed well away from any large centres of population: a number of sites were considered around Leeds, but Thorp Arch was chosen.

Thorp Arch may have solved the question of safety, but it created another problem: a large workforce was required at the factory, but where would they come from and how could they be transported? The solution was to recruit or even conscript staff, many of them women, from around Leeds and surrounding West Riding towns, and to

transport them by rail to the local railway station – then known as "Thorp Arch for Boston Spa" – which was situated on the line between Harrogate and Church Fenton. Initially, this was reasonably successful but the numbers employed continued to grow as production increased, and the number of trains required far exceeded the capacity of the line, which was also acting as one of the routes carrying coal from the North East to the Midlands.

Furthermore, in order to minimise the consequences of an explosion, the factory had been built as a series of small buildings over a large site. The solution was to build a single track railway, running north of the Church Fenton route, then in a large circle connecting four stations which were conveniently located around the factory, before returning to the main line just west of the viaduct over the River Wharfe. Overall, the running line was about three and a half miles long.

The original signal box at Thorp Arch, adjacent

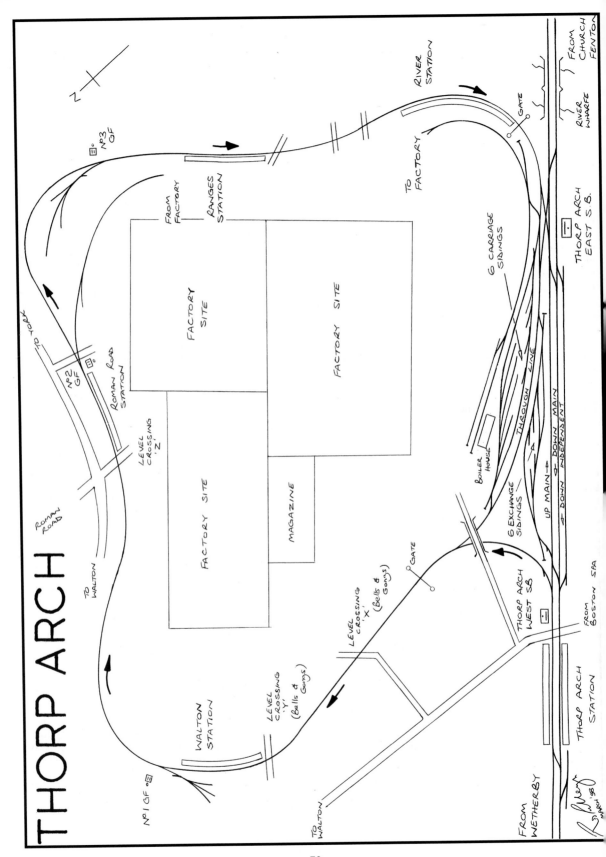

THORP ARCH

to the station and level crossing, was extended to control the western junction, and renamed Thorp Arch West. At the eastern junction, a new brick signal box, Thorp Arch East, was constructed by the L.N.E.R. to its typical wartime pattern, with minimal windows and flat roof.

The line was fully opened on Sunday 19 April 1942. Trains could enter the Circular Railway from either the east or the west, then run in a clockwise direction to Thorp Arch East where the junction faced west only; trains departing for the Church Fenton direction had to reverse direction on the Through Line between East and West before proceeding. Between the two signal boxes on the Up side, were extensive carriage sidings; on the Down side a new Independent running line was installed.

The main running line on the Circular Railway was track circuited throughout, with colour light signals to control the trains automatically; interestingly, in order to reduce costs, and overcome the lack of suitable parts, some of the signal heads were mounted on second hand concrete posts or even on old telegraph poles cut back to the appropriate height.

Stations were provided at Walton, Roman Road, Ranges and River. Each consisted of a long, single platform with at least one shelter, and dimmed electric lighting.

Ground frames controlled connections to an internal rail system which served various parts of the factory. An engine shed, close to Walton station, provided accommodation for the locomotives used on the internal system: these included five Fowler diesel shunters and one oil fired Hunslet Saddle Tank.

At its peak, the factory was working around the clock; up to 18,000 workers were employed, with three shift changes through the day. Trains ran non-stop along the Wetherby line until they reached the Circular Railway where they called at all four stations, before entering the carriage sidings; shift changes then took place in the factory, following which the empty trains ran out of the Carriage Sidings, round the circuit for the second time, then away to their destinations.

The factory remained operational well after the Second World War for a variety of purposes, including storage and manufacture of ammunition for the Korean War.

By 1956, trains were still running to and from Hull, Leeds, Normanton and Harrogate, although none of these trains were shown in the public timetable.

Interestingly, again because of security, the line never appeared on Ordnance Survey maps.

The last train ran on 15 August 1958, following which the Circular Railway was closed and today there is very little physical evidence that there was once an extensive railway network on the estate.

On 8 June 1958, the Thorp Arch Circular Railway was traversed by the RCTS Roses Rail Tour. This colour light signal appears to be mounted on a proper post. *(Peter Sunderland)*

Emergency Diversionary Route
By Richard D. Pulleyn

On 18 February 1967, DP2 was in charge of the 'White Rose Pullman' from King's Cross to Bradford and Harrogate. It has run round at Leeds Central and is ready to depart with the front portion for Bradford Exchange. *(D. J. Mitchell)*

Monday 31 July 1967 was dry and bright. At Skelton signal box, on the East Coast Mainline just north of York, the 2.40a.m. Cliffe–Uddingston block cement train was routed along the Down Slow to keep it out of the path of the 12.00noon Kings Cross to Edinburgh express, which left York at 2.57p.m.

In charge of the express that day was locomotive DP2 – so named because it was the second Deltic Prototype – in fact it had been a last minute substitute for the rostered Deltic shortly before leaving Kings Cross.

All appeared well as the express accelerated along the Down Fast until, just south of Thirsk, the driver became aware of a large dust cloud ahead. This was caused by the cement train which had broken in two, both portions being derailed. An emergency brake application was made on board DP2, but it was too late and the powerful diesel locomotive struck the cement wagons a glancing blow causing derailment and severe damage. The following coaches also struck the debris; sadly, as a consequence, seven passengers were killed and 45 were injured.

The Down Slow, Down Fast and Up Fast were all completely blocked. Only the Up Slow was clear – provided that trains passed with extreme caution.

The 10.27a.m. Bristol–Newcastle had already left York but was brought to a stand at Pilmoor where the locomotive had to run round its train before returning to York.

At York station, emergency procedures were quickly brought into operation: trains from the north were badly delayed but still managing to get through. Emergency Single Line Working by Pilotman was introduced temporarily over the Up Slow between Thirsk and Pilmoor, past the scene of the accident. However, most trains from London, Liverpool, Bristol and Poole had to be terminated at York and a bus service was introduced to convey passengers to Thirsk where rail connections were provided.

The 2.00p.m. and 4.00p.m. expresses from Kings Cross were diverted via the Settle–Carlisle and Waverley routes, but both passenger and freight traffic for the north was building up on the approaches to York and delays were becoming significant.

Attention then turned to the line from Harrogate to Northallerton. Although this had closed to passenger traffic some four months earlier – with effect from Monday 6 March 1967 – it had remained open from Starbeck for a daily freight train which ran to Ripon and, as required, through to the Ministry of Defence depot at Melmerby. Most of the signalling

DP2 travelling on the down fast line has struck the derailed wagons of the cement train on the down slow and has been deflected over towards the up fast line. *(John M. Boyes)*

A closer view of the damaged passenger coaches and cement wagons south of Thirsk on 31 July 1967. *(John M. Boyes)*

equipment on the line was intact but had not been used for almost five months. The daily trip was worked both ways over the former Up line under "One-Engine-in-Steam" Regulations, with a Travelling Signalman accompanying each train to work the level crossing gates by wheel and authorise the driver to pass signals at danger. There was no traffic at all between Melmerby and Northallerton.

Whilst the engineers and operating staff from York busied themselves with repairing the ECML, the team from Darlington despatched a test train along the Leeds Northern from the Northallerton end. The train was formed from an engine and a couple of vans containing batteries and sundry equipment to restore the block signalling. By 6.45p.m., less than four hours after the smash, the Ripon line was passed as fit for use, although a 30m.p.h. speed limit was imposed north of Melmerby.

The following signal boxes (SBs) and gate boxes (GBs) between Starbeck and Northallerton were reopened and remanned.

Bilton SB, Nidd Bridge SB, Wormald Green SB, Littlethorpe SB, Melmerby North SB, Middleton Green Lane GB, Pickhill SB, Maunby GB, and Newby Wiske SB. Initially, the signal box at Ripon remained switched out of circuit because there was no level crossing to be supervised and there were only sufficient signalling staff to operate essential locations.

The signal boxes and gate boxes between York and Starbeck were already open, but arrangements had to be made for 24 hour working, mostly achieved by staff working 12 hour shifts.

At first, trains from Starbeck northwards had to be worked by the "Time Interval and Caution Ticket" system but, as the signal engineers worked hard to install new batteries at each location, full block working was eventually restored over the Down line; the Up line was not required because traffic was flowing over the Up Slow south of Thirsk.

Between three and four trains per hour followed each other over the Down line between Starbeck and Northallerton: as one train cleared the section in advance, the next was standing ready to follow. The local freight trip working to Ripon and Melmerby was cancelled on Tuesday 1 August to keep the line clear for passenger traffic.

Passenger expresses and some higher classification freights were given priority right through until 6.00a.m. on Wednesday 2 August, by which time limited traffic was once again flowing along the ECML. Nevertheless, a number of freights continued to be diverted via Ripon up until 12 noon.

At lunchtime on 2 August, the Starbeck-Melmerby freight went out to Ripon, returning at teatime – thus becoming the only train signalled over the Up line after block working was resumed. The following day, "One-Engine-in-Steam" working was resumed south of Melmerby and peace descended once more on this former major trunk line.

Some cited the diversion as justification for re-opening the route permanently, but this was not to be. By early 1968, an overbridge at Sinderby was deemed unsafe and filled in without even removing the track which remained in situ. The remaining signalling was taken out of use on 28 May 1969 and removed shortly afterwards. The last freight ran on 3 October 1969, and the track was finally lifted in 1970.

Nidd Bridge looking north in November 1966. The station had closed in 1962 but the line was then still fully open. *(P. B. Booth/N. E. Stead Collection)*

Class B16 No.61412 heads a southbound freight through Pickhill about 1955. This station remained open until 1959 but latterly had only a token passenger service. *(J. W. Hague/N. E. Stead Collection)*

Preserved K4 No.3442 'The Great Marquess' and A3 No.4472 'Flying Scotsman' about to cross Bilton Viaduct with a special from London to Darlington on 3 October 1964. *(David Beeken)*

A class 45 'Peak' arrives at Northallerton with the 9.55a.m. Newcastle to Liverpool Lime Street via York. The dmu in the bay platform forms the connecting service to Leeds via Ripon and Harrogate on Sunday 5 March 1967.

(Charles Allenby)

The same three car Metro Cammell set pauses at Ripon on this, the last day of service.
(Charles Allenby)

Closure to passengers on 6 March did not prevent the Duke of Edinburgh travelling in the Royal Train to Nidd Bridge on 30 May 1967. 'Jubilee' class No.45562 'Alberta' hauled the train from York via Starbeck then empty to Ripon to run round and tender first back to York.

(Stephen Middleton)

Trans Pennine to Harrogate?

In Volume Two of *Railways in East Yorkshire*, I described the evolution of the 'Trans Pennine Express' network. Broadly speaking, this had reached the stage by 1994 of four hourly trains running from Blackpool, Liverpool, Manchester Piccadilly and Manchester Airport to Scarborough, Newcastle, Hull and Middlesbrough.

It is part of the franchise agreement that, by May 2000, line capacity permitting, there should be a fifth hourly express across the Pennines.

Most of the trains comprise air conditioned class 158 units. Part of the success of the service has been in extending trains of this quality through to places such as Scarborough, Middlesbrough and Sunderland which previously saw only connecting local trains.

York has gained enormously from the expansion of the 'Trans Pennine' concept. At present (1998/9) it has three expresses per hour to Leeds which go forward to Blackpool, Liverpool and Manchester Airport. When the 'Trans Pennine' brand name was first introduced in 1961, the two Newcastle-Liverpool expresses routed via York didn't even stop there. At that time, York had no regular through trains beyond Leeds.

By contrast, Harrogate stands out as possibly the most important town which has not benefited from these developments. Back in 1961, Harrogate was served by two Newcastle to Liverpool expresses. The following year it also gained an hourly through service to Manchester via the Calder Valley employing what were then considered to be superior diesel multiple units.

Today, Harrogate has to rely on its half hourly all stations service to Leeds and hourly local to York.

The failure of either the Newcastle or Middlesbrough trains to serve Harrogate is obviously due to closure of the route through Ripon in 1967. But surely that doesn't condemn Harrogate to rely solely on local trains on its surviving line.

If there is to be an additional express each hour between Manchester Piccadilly and Leeds, then surely it would be overkill for it to continue to York, superimposed on the present service of at least three expresses and one local each hour. Would it not make more sense to consider running it to Harrogate with stops only at Horsforth and Hornbeam Park, the two busiest intermediate stations.

As well as affording Harrogate a through service to Manchester, this would give superior rolling stock and an accelerated schedule for at least some passengers beginning their journeys at Harrogate for other destinations.

A predecessor to today's 'Trans Pennine' express, the Sunday 5.00p.m. Manchester Exchange to Newcastle is seen just north of Horsforth behind A4 No.60005 'Sir Charles Newton' on 26 May 1957.

(B. K. B. Green)

D278 is signalled onto the Wetherby branch as it passes through Cross Gates with the 11a.m. Liverpool Lime Street to Newcastle via Harrogate in August 1961. This was the first year of the Trans Pennine diesel service and a few trains were routed via Wetherby to avoid reversal in Leeds now that there was no need to change engines there.

(Peter Sunderland)

Previously these trains had generally run via Arthington as reversal in Leeds City was no problem given that the locos would be changed anyway. V2 No.60928 has the 8.55a.m. Newcastle to Liverpool Lime Street on 24 May 1958. *(M. Mitchell)*

158813 prepares to leave Newcastle for Liverpool Lime Street on 4 May 1998. If the Ripon line had survived, then this train might well be routed via Harrogate.

(Martin Bairstow)

Rights of Way

Most railways were laid on extremely well engineered alignments. One might have thought that these rights of way were national assets worth far more as complete routes than their mere scrap value in bits. Yet when the greatest number of railway closures took place in the 1960s, there was no facility to consider whether the trackbeds might have a future use either as railways or anything else. They were just broken up and offered for sale piecemeal. In the case of all the closed lines radiating from Harrogate, traffic at the time of closure was either minimal or capable of being re-routed elsewhere. But that did not mean, or should not have meant, that there was no possibility of their having a future use. Had the rights of way been protected, then there is a real possibility that today there would be commuter trains between Leeds and Wetherby and maybe between Leeds and Otley, perhaps also between Harrogate and Ripon. It is also very likely that the Ripley to Pateley Bridge route would by now have been developed as a footpath and cycle way.

Instead, most of the formations were destroyed. Where lengths of route have survived it is usually because no purchaser could be found for them. Only recently has attention focused on the potential of those bits which remain.

Two sections of route have been converted for walkers and cyclists. One is from Wetherby to Spofforth including all three sides of the Wetherby triangle. The other is from both Dragon Junction and Starbeck North through Bilton Junction to the south end of Bilton Viaduct. The most intensive traffic on this latter route is people walking dogs near Bilton Junction. Evidence of the popularity of this facility is there for all to see and tread in.

Examples of railways converted into roads are comparatively rare because they are generally not wide enough. The Otley bypass does follow the trackbed of the railway for about one mile passing through the station site which had been completely obliterated.

The light engine is coming from Church Fenton direction. The line from Wetherby Station curves in on the right.
(Martin Bairstow)

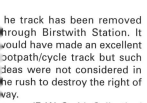

The track has been removed through Birstwith Station. It would have made an excellent footpath/cycle track but such ideas were not considered in the rush to destroy the right of way.

(F. W. Smith Collection)

The River Wharfe bridge, north of Collingham, being demolished in August 1967.
(M. Mitchell)

The axe falls on Otley Station and signal box.
(F. W. Smith Collection)

Then the track is taken away by the demolition train. This is now the route of the Otley bypass.
(F. W. Smith Collection)